WOODTURNING
JEWELLERY

WOODTURNING
JEWELLERY

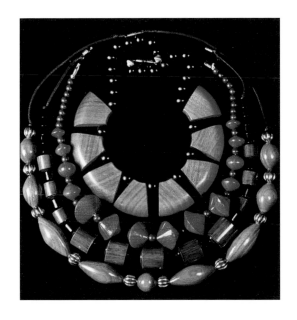

HILARY BOWEN

GUILD OF MASTER CRAFTSMAN PUBLICATIONS

First published 1995 by
Guild of Master Craftsman Publications Ltd,
166 High Street, Lewes,
East Sussex BN7 1XU

© Hilary Bowen 1995

ISBN 0 946819 83 1

Photographs © Hilary Bowen 1995
Illustrations © Tim Benké 1995

Designed by Ian Hunt Design
Printed and bound in Hong Kong
under the supervision of Mandarin Offset, London

Acknowledgements

Special thanks to Bob Carabine for his tolerance, patience, ideas and encouragement.

Grateful thanks to all those people (particularly members of the Hampshire Woodturners' Association) who have given me advice, tips and information along the way. Thanks also to Jim Gilbert for starting me off on the road to woodturning and for his encouragement during my formative period.

CONTENTS

Introduction

'A thing of beauty is a joy forever.' (Keats, 1818)

OVER THE LAST FEW YEARS woodturning has become a fast-growing leisure activity, particularly in the UK, parts of Europe, North America, Australia and New Zealand, and there is a corresponding growth industry in books and magazines devoted entirely to the subject. After starting woodturning as a hobby a few years ago, I decided I would like to combine an existing interest in jewellery with my new interest, and began to look for any literature on woodturned jewellery. My quest was short-lived, because there seemed to have been very little written on the subject. Consequently, most of the techniques offered in this book I have developed through experimentation. Talking to people, finding occasional articles in magazines, and using a system of trial and error, have all helped.

So why has so little been written on the subject of woodturned jewellery? I think the answer may lie in the very diverse origins of woodturning and jewellery manufacture. Traditionally, woodturners earned a living by making functional items such as bowls, goblets, tool handles and so forth, which were relatively quick to make and cheap to buy. Woodturning as a hobby is a comparatively recent phenomenon, and has come about, like so many other hobbies, as a result of increased leisure time over the past few decades. And only recently has it become accepted that woodturning can be an *art form*, rather than simply a craft, producing objects that have no practical function, and which are purely ornamental. Woodturned jewellery, then, is perhaps a logical extension of this development.

In complete contrast, jewellery has traditionally been made from precious and semi-precious metals and stones; in other words, materials chosen for their colour, lustre and durability. In comparison with precious metals, polished stones, ceramics and glass, wood has always been considered a poor man's alternative.

In this book, however, I hope to illustrate that wood is, in fact, an ideal material for jewellery. It, too, has a lustre and a richness of colour which, when combined with suitable shape and form, can produce an effect that is both stunning and beautiful.

This book is not intended for complete beginners, but for those whose level of skill might be described as 'novice' to 'intermediate'. A basic knowledge of turning processes and tool use is essential, and a basic level of skill is assumed. However, no techniques are described that are particularly difficult for anyone who has mastered the basics.

Many of the projects outlined in this book will also appeal to people who lack a great deal of time. Most of the basic items can be made fairly quickly. After that, it is up to the individual how much time is spent upon further decoration. By and large, the items described tend to be fun to make and also make ideal presents.

Part One of this book is concerned with some points to be considered before beginning to make an object. These include safety precautions, selection of timber, design, and so forth. Part Two consists of chapters showing how to make specific items: earrings, brooches, bangles, rings and necklaces. Part Three looks at a variety of ways of enhancing the appearance of wooden jewellery: stains and dyes, inlaying wire, laminating, colouring, beading, and finishing, etc.

Acknowledging that there are more ways than one of achieving the same result, I rarely recommend the use of a specific tool (unless there is no alternative), as different turners will have their own preferred tools and techniques for making a particular cut. For the same reason, I rarely give a specific lathe speed, preferring to let the individual decide for him or herself the appropriate speed and tool. Indeed, it is very likely that some readers will choose to carry out a procedure using a completely different method to one I have outlined – I have simply described the methods which *I* find the most straightforward.

This book is essentially a collection of *ideas*, and I hope that these ideas will encourage the individual turner to experiment further, and to discover variations on the basic theme. The chapters in Part Three are intended to help this process.

Finally, I have also tried to emphasize that it is possible to produce attractive, high-quality items *cheaply*. Chapter 3, for example, explores the possibilities of obtaining timber from cheap sources. Since only small pieces of wood are needed for jewellery, it is not necessary to spend huge amounts of money on timber. Indeed, offcuts are often ideal.

Similarly, I have tried to emphasize the fact that expensive equipment is not needed. Apart from basic pieces of major equipment, such as a lathe, bandsaw, etc., only basic tools and chucks are required. All the methods described require only the most simple equipment and techniques. These projects, therefore, are ideal for people trying to manage on a limited budget, and with a minimum of equipment and storage space.

At the beginning of each chapter there is a list of 'essential' equipment and a list of 'recommended' equipment, the latter referring to equipment that is very useful to have but not absolutely necessary. I have also given an indication of the level of skill required. This varies throughout from 'novice' to 'intermediate'.

Finally, I would like to reiterate the importance of experimentation. There is no end to the variety of designs that can be produced through these few basic techniques. The only limit is our own imagination!

PART ONE

Preliminaries

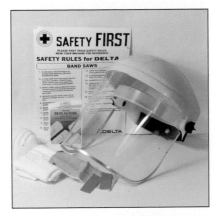

Health and Safety

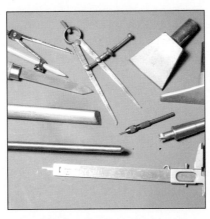

Tools and Equipment

Timber

Chucking Techniques

Design

CHAPTER

1
Health and Safety

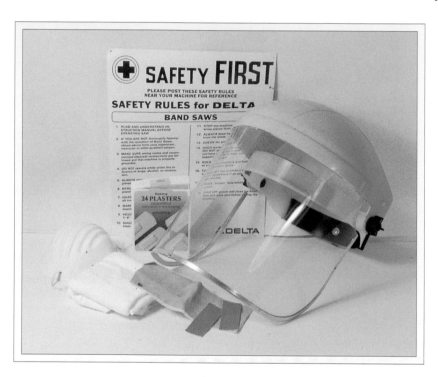

- Face protection
- Respiratory protection
- Tool storage
- Clothing
- Mental attitude

Because non-professional turners are not bound by statutory regulations on health and safety, it is particularly important that they ensure they are not working in a potentially hazardous environment. As a general rule, it is a good idea to keep a first-aid box in the workshop so that items such as sticking plasters, bandages, and so forth are near to hand, should they be needed.

FACE PROTECTION

Face protection is absolutely essential. It is not enough to wear protective goggles alone since, although they will offer some protection to the eyes, they cannot shield the rest of the face which is vulnerable to stray flying chips (or worse). When worn in conjunction with a dust mask to protect the nose and mouth, goggles tend to steam up, rendering them useless.

At the very least, a full-face safety helmet should be used. This is lightweight and offers protection for the whole face. It is comfortable to wear and gives a sense of greater safety generally, which can be beneficial. A disposable dust mask can be worn at the same time without the visor steaming up.

RESPIRATORY PROTECTION

A safety helmet on its own does not protect against the inhalation of fine dust, which is a renowned health hazard. Disposable dust masks do offer some protection but they have a limited life and are less effective against very fine dust, especially over long periods.

There are now a number of devices on the market which offer respiratory as well as facial protection. Half-mask respirators are face units fitted with a disposable cartridge filter. Although the filters need to be replaced at intervals, they last longer than ordinary dust masks. Powered respirators are more expensive but offer the best protection of all. They are a complete unit, providing a

continuous supply of filtered air over the face. The internal fan is battery-driven, and the batteries last between eight and twelve hours in most models. Finally, for regular and frequent users of a lathe or bandsaw, the possibility of installing a general dust extractor should be explored.

In addition to the general hazards caused by breathing in fine dust, it should be remembered that many woods (especially the tropical varieties) can cause allergic reactions in some people. Such reactions typically include respiratory problems and skin irritations. These can vary in severity, depending on the species of wood and the individual's sensitivity to it. Most turners find that there are one or two woods that they simply cannot turn because of these allergies.

TOOL STORAGE

While this may not at first seem to be connected with health and safety, there are considerable potential hazards related to the storage of tools. The first consideration is the storage of small hand tools near large pieces of machinery. Machines such as lathes, bandsaws and pillar drills should never have untidy racks of hand tools stored above them. It is all too easy for a screwdriver or a pair of pliers to fall accidentally from the rack onto a machine while it is switched on (or prior to use), with disastrous consequences if it were to become entangled with the working mechanisms. Those obliged to work in cramped conditions and who must have tool racks close to machinery should ensure that the tools are always secure within their rack.

It is also important to have adequate storage systems so that there is less temptation to leave tools lying around on work surfaces where they can fall off or get inadvertently pushed into, onto or under machinery. Such systems do not need to be expensive ready-made tool racks or boxes. Small cardboard or plastic boxes, shelves drilled with appropriately sized holes, pinboards, hooks and other similar devices can be used to provide storage space where tools are safe and easily accessible.

It is also advisable to establish routines for replacing small items after use. It is very easy to forget to remove the chuck key from a pillar drill, for example, prior to drilling. This can be extremely dangerous, but is so easily done. As human beings we are all prone to absent-mindedness and it is this that causes so many accidents.

General tidiness in the workshop is also important. Lathes produce vast quantities of shavings beneath which things can quickly become buried. At best, this is an irritation. At worst, it can result in injury by treading on pieces of waste wood thrown carelessly onto the floor. Ankles have been twisted and broken due to scraps of wood hidden under shavings. Always have a container handy into which offcuts can be thrown.

CLOTHING

This is largely common sense, but it is worth emphasizing the importance of wearing suitable clothing in the workplace. There should be no loose ends, such as ties or undone cuffs, which could become caught in machinery. Long hair should be tied back at all times.

MENTAL ATTITUDE

Unlike professional woodturners who are obliged to turn for long hours on a daily basis, people who turn wood for a hobby can at least choose when they want to turn (within the constraints of their free time). In order to prevent accidents happening through tiredness or general lack of attention, it is wise to try to avoid turning late in the evening or for long stretches without a break. Set realistic targets so that you do not need to rush. Impatience can often result in poor quality work and, in some cases, accidents. Give yourself enough time to do a job properly. Glue should be left to set properly, sanding should be done thoroughly, the lathe may need a period of time to cool down, and so forth.

Above all, if things are not going well and you feel yourself becoming angry or frustrated, then stop. It is much better to stop what you are doing and continue another day than to persevere, taking out your anger on the wood. Remember that everybody has days when nothing seems to go right and this is especially true with woodturning. To return to the task another day in a more positive frame of mind will usually prove to be the best course.

CHAPTER

2
Tools and Equipment

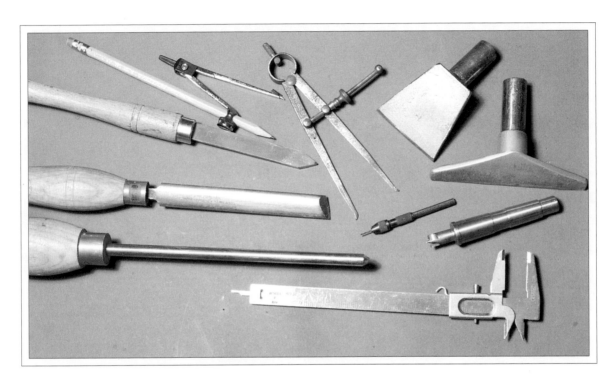

■ Essential and non-
  essential equipment
■ Purchasing equipment
■ Basic machinery

■ Turning tools
■ Turning accessories
■ Hand tools
■ Adhesives

Peorle who rely on their craft alone for their income are rarely wealthy, and woodturners are no exception. Perhaps this is why, traditionally, woodturners are good at making inexpensive jigs and devices and making do with what they have. This applies not only to professionals but also to amateurs who pursue woodturning as a hobby. Even the most unsophisticated lathe represents a considerable outlay of money, and tools are also expensive.

ESSENTIAL AND NON-ESSENTIAL EQUIPMENT

This chapter lists items that are essential for producing jewellery, and distinguishes them from the equipment that is merely useful. Tools that can be made or adapted simply and cheaply are also included.

I will not recommend any particular manufacturers of machinery. Ultimately it comes down to personal preference and size of budget. It is also true that, to a certain extent, you get what you pay for and that by paying a higher price you often get better quality. However, in some instances a higher price can reflect a better-known brand name, or perhaps extra features or gadgets that you may hardly ever need to use.

PURCHASING EQUIPMENT

Before buying any major piece of equipment, it is worth exploring the market carefully to make sure you know exactly what you need. Talk to other people, read magazine articles that compare different models, go to shows that give demonstrations, and then having decided on what you want, see if you can find any special offers. There are many discount prices available if you look around. It is also possible to get hold of ex-demonstration models that have been used for a few days at shows. These nearly brand-new pieces of equipment are often sold off at good prices.

Many magazines advertise second-hand equipment, which can be a good way of acquiring what you need, particularly since it can enable you to buy better quality items than you would be able to afford brand new. However, remember that you get no guarantee when purchasing equipment in this way and you would need to get it checked over very carefully from a safety point of view. You do not know how the previous owner may have mistreated your piece of machinery, and alterations may have been made that could reduce its safety. Also, general wear and tear may have affected its performance.

BASIC MACHINERY

LATHE

As most of the jewellery described in this book is turned, a lathe is essential, although a very basic model is adequate. Nothing of a large diameter is to be turned, so neither an outboard facility nor swivel-head is necessary: the items can be turned on the most simple of inexpensive lathes, with no additional features.

TOOL GRINDER

This is essential, but need not be expensive – I have been happily using one of the cheapest models on the market for quite some time. Of course, like anything else, it depends what you want out of it, but for basic tool sharpening a big outlay is not necessary. It is important to remember, though, that very sharp tools are absolutely essential for the procedures described in this book, so whatever you use, it must be capable of giving you a really good edge.

BANDSAW

Strictly speaking, this is not absolutely essential, and I managed without one for quite a long time. Having said that, it is difficult and time-consuming to saw up small pieces of wood by hand, so a bandsaw is recommended. It not only makes life easier and saves time, it also saves wood, as irregular pieces of wood can be sawn into regular turning blanks, which would have been impossible by hand. Offcuts become more accessible, and you may find yourself keeping pieces that would otherwise have been thrown away.

Because blanks for jewellery tend to be very small, it is wise to take extra special care when using a bandsaw, mainly because one's fingers tend to be that much nearer the blade than with larger blanks. If the piece of wood to be sawn is particularly small, or of an irregular shape, it is often advisable to construct a simple jig to carry it through the blade.

One job for which a bandsaw is absolutely essential is for sawing thin laminates (*see* Chapter 13). When cutting along the grain, it is important to use as wide a blade as possible, and to ensure that it is perfectly sharp. A thin or blunt blade will sometimes result in a crooked cut, due to the blade wandering along the grain.

Unfortunately, even the cheapest bandsaws are quite expensive, but you can at least choose one from the cheaper end of the market. It is a good idea, though, to think carefully about the size of stock that you are likely to want to cut. You may not always be wanting to cut small pieces. The depth of cut is an important factor to take into account when choosing a bandsaw and it is probably sensible to buy one with as large a depth of cut as you can afford. Five inches is adequate for most non-professionals, and is more than adequate for making blanks for jewellery.

It should be emphasized that adherence to the safety instructions supplied with the machine is essential at all times. Although the bandsaw can be considered a potentially dangerous machine, it is, like a car, as safe as its user. In the right hands it is perfectly safe provided the safety precautions are followed. Most accidents tend to occur if the user is in a hurry or has become a little over-confident and careless.

Fig 2.1

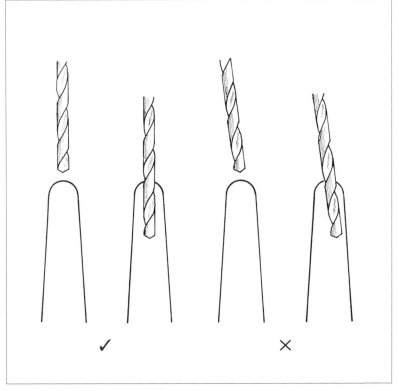

Figs 2.1 and 2.2 Holes must be drilled vertically.   Fig 2.2

PILLAR DRILL
(OR DRILL PRESS)

This is by no means essential, and as far as the jewellery in this book is concerned, it is possible to manage quite easily without one. Nevertheless, if your budget allows it, there are times when it can be extremely useful, especially for drilling very small holes through the stems of long, thin earrings. However, even this operation can be achieved with a hand drill provided the work is suitably clamped in position and you have a steady hand. The main advantage of a pillar drill for this type of work is that it enables holes to be drilled that are exactly vertical, and this can be crucial for thin-stemmed earrings. To drill a hole at a slight angle through the end of a long-stemmed earring could result in the drill point breaking through the stem slightly below the point of entry, thus ruining the piece (*see* Figs 2.1 and 2.2). A drill stand for work of this kind would be a cheaper alternative to a pillar drill.

TURNING TOOLS

It is a popular misconception that miniature turning tools are needed for turning small objects such as jewellery. Although there are times when a small tool can be particularly useful for getting access to small crevices, by and large they are not really necessary. Having said that, some people do prefer to use them for small work and later in this chapter I will be describing how to make your own set.

The basic turning tools that I would recommend are as follows:

▌ A roughing gouge
▌ A bowl gouge ground to a fingernail shape at the end
▌ A parting tool
▌ A small scraper
▌ A skew chisel

All of these tools should be medium size. Anything else is really a bonus, although most people have one or two preferred tools that they use more than others. In my experience, one's choice of tool for certain procedures is not critical. Most turners tend to use the tools with which they feel most comfortable, and which do the job reasonably well. In addition to the basic range, it does help to have a few other tools from time to time for specific jobs, but it is often possible to make or adapt your own. For example, I have some very small scrapers

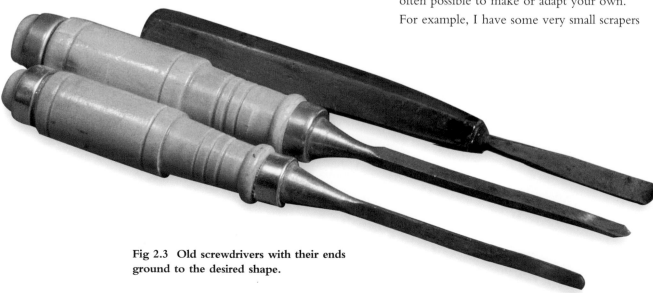

Fig 2.3 Old screwdrivers with their ends ground to the desired shape.

which were originally old large screwdrivers with strong shanks and fairly long handles. I re-ground the ends to produce scrapers, one with a rounded blunt end, for example, and another with a slightly pointed end for getting into small spaces (*see* Fig 2.3). The tool that I have found to be most versatile is a ⅜in (10mm) deep-fluted bowl gouge ground to a steep angle. I probably use this more than any other tool, simply because I find it comfortable, versatile and easy to use.

Of the skew chisels, I would recommend an oval skew. As the name suggests, this is one with an oval cross section (*see* Fig 2.4). The advantage of this over the type with a rectangular cross section is that it is easier to roll on the tool rest since it has no corners and, in this way, a smoother action can be achieved. For jewellery and any other small work it is essential to have a thin skew chisel

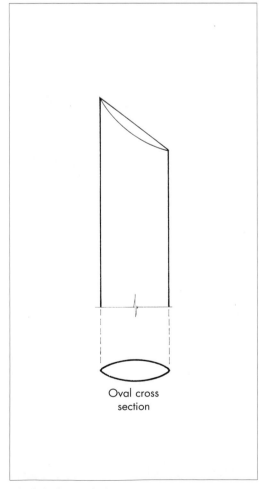

Fig 2.4 An oval skew.

for getting into small spaces, when parting off, for example, or when making small beads.

MAKING A SET OF MINIATURE TURNING TOOLS

As mentioned earlier, miniature turning tools are not essential. Indeed, some turners claim that larger tools are preferable even for small work because they have greater stability and therefore reduce 'chatter'. However, for those who find small tools easier when working with small items, it is possible to make one's own set of basic miniature turning tools, both simply and cheaply.

Begin by turning the handles to the required width and length. Make sure that the handles are long enough to be used comfortably, safely, and with adequate support. Use short pieces of copper piping from plumbers' merchants for the ferrules. Hammer a large masonry nail vertically into the end of each handle, then grind off the heads. The ends can then be ground into any desired shape, according to your needs (*see* Fig 2.5).

Of course, there is a limit to the type of tool that can be made in this way. Obviously, fluted gouges are out of the question, but small scrapers and chisels can be made quite adequately (*see* Fig 2.6). Old dental instruments can also be utilized, by grinding the ends to the required shape.

TURNING ACCESSORIES

SHORT TOOL REST

It is difficult to get commercially produced tool rests smaller than 4½in (114mm), and I find that even this size is too long for making many items of jewellery. I have had a tool rest specially made that is approximately 2½in (64mm) in length (*see* Fig 2.7). This is very useful since it enables the rest to fit in close to the wood. It is by no means essential to have such a short tool rest, but if you are able to make one or acquire one, it can be an advantage.

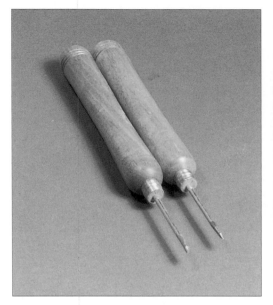

Fig 2.5

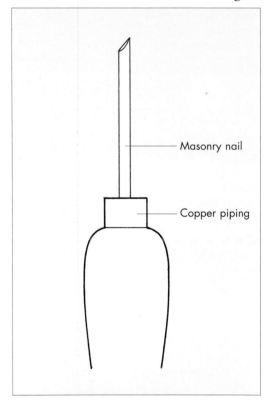

Masonry nail

Copper piping

Fig 2.7 **A short tool rest.**

Fig 2.8 **A miniature four-prong drive centre.**

Figs 2.5 and 2.6 Home-made miniature turning tools.   Fig 2.6

MINIATURE DRIVE CENTRE

Again, this is not essential, but it is useful. These drive centres are primarily designed for turning small stock. The four-prong drive centre has a diameter small enough to turn square stock of less than ⅜in (10mm) in cross section (see Fig 2.8).

STANDARD DRILL CHUCK

A standard drill chuck on a morse taper that can be fitted into the headstock of the lathe is not essential, but it can be useful sometimes as an alternative method of holding small section stock, such as lace bobbin blanks.

CONTRACTING COLLET CHUCK

This is very useful for holding spigots when making items such as brooches. It would be ideal to have various sizes, but the most useful size would be one that contracts down to about ¾-½in (20-25mm). Again, this is not essential, but it is *extremely* useful.

Alternatively, a small cup chuck or jam chuck would do the job, though with less versatility.

EXPANDING DOVETAIL COLLET

Again, this is not absolutely essential, but it is very useful when turning bangles since it enables the bangle to be accurately reverse-chucked. These chucks come in a variety of sizes but one with an expanding diameter of approximately 2½in (64mm) is ideal for bangles.

HAND TOOLS

The following is a list of small hand tools that I have found to be either essential or just very useful:

PIN VICE AND MINIATURE DRILL BITS

If you wish to make long, thin-stemmed earrings that require a small hole in the end of the shaft, then a set of miniature drill bits (or even just one) is essential. You will need a drill that is between 0.03 and 0.04in (0.8 and 1mm), depending on the width of the wire to be inserted into the hole. The problem with drills of this size is that they do tend to break rather easily so it is a good idea to keep a spare one in reserve. Since drills of this width are too narrow to be held in a conventional drill chuck, you will need a pin vice. This is a miniature screw chuck small enough to grip the drill bit (*see* Fig 2.9). Once the drill bit has been inserted, the pin

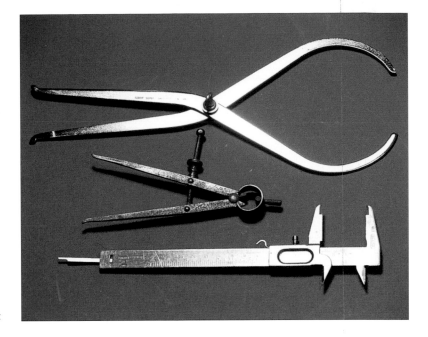

vice is itself then fitted into the drill chuck on the electric drill in the usual way. It can be used both with hand-held electric drills and with pillar drills. Pin vices come in different sizes according to the size of the drill bit to be held. For most jewellery work, since very small drill bits are used, it is necessary to ensure that the pin vice is small enough to close down completely, otherwise it will not hold the drill bit.

CALLIPERS

Callipers are essential when making jewellery, for ensuring that rings or bangles fit, for making a pair of earrings that match, and for countless other procedures. They are relatively inexpensive, and can even be picked up second-hand at jumble sales, car-boot sales etc.

Callipers are tools for measuring small distances, for example the width or length of a small object. There are various types of calliper, each designed to do a specific job. Internal callipers (*see* Fig 2.11) are designed to measure internal widths, for example the inside diameter of a bangle. External callipers (*see* Fig 2.12) measure outside widths, for example the diameter of an earring. It is also possible to buy 'inside-outside' callipers, which do both jobs (*see* Fig 2.13).

Fig 2.10 A selection of callipers.

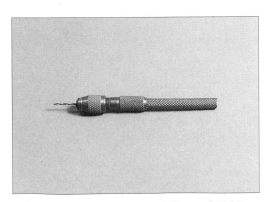

Fig 2.9 A pin vice with a miniature drill bit.

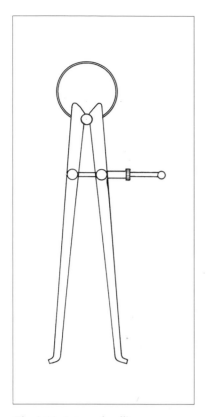

Fig 2.11 Internal callipers.

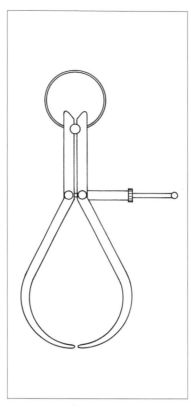

Fig 2.12 External callipers.

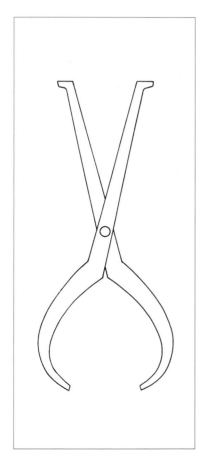

Fig 2.13 Inside-outside callipers.

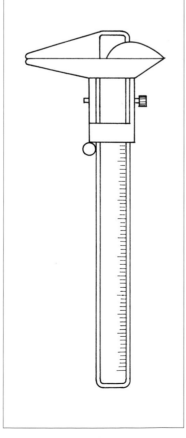

Fig 2.14 Slide callipers.

Slide callipers (*see* Fig 2.14) are also useful since they give an exact measurement on a calibrated scale, and (like the inside-outside callipers) they are so designed that the inside jaw distance exactly equals the outside jaw distance, making them ideal for turning spigots, matching recesses, or making rings, for example. They also have a depth gauge.

A profile gauge (*see* Fig 2.15) can sometimes be useful, especially for people who find it difficult to copy shapes by eye. The only disadvantage for jewellery work is that the distance between the headstock and the tailstock is usually less than the overall length of the profile gauge and so most of them are too long to be held against the work while it is mounted between centres. Nevertheless, they can prove quite useful at times.

MINI-HACKSAW

Although not absolutely essential, mini-hacksaws are very useful and are relatively cheap, so it is worth getting one. I use mine a lot, for all sorts of things. A useful type to buy is one with interchangeable woodcutting and metal cutting blades. On particularly small items I tend to use the metal cutting blade because the wood blades can sometimes be too coarse for really delicate operations.

ADHESIVES

This is another area in which people tend to have different personal preferences, and about which there are few hard and fast rules. There are a number of essential factors that will determine the type of glue to be used:

REQUIRED STRENGTH OF BOND
For really strong bonds, a PVA woodworking glue can be used, though Cascamite is better and is particularly suitable for laminates. This is because it is fully waterproof and highly stable. Unlike PVA glues, the joints will not 'creep' with

Cascamite. Its disadvantage is that it has a long drying time and should ideally be left overnight, so forward planning is needed.

Cyanoacrylate glues (which are usually marketed under the generic heading of 'superglue') can form a very strong bond. Epoxy resin is also very good for small areas.

Sometimes only a medium-strength bond is required. For example, when gluing together two halves of a rectangular blank (with a layer of paper in between) to be split later after turning, a medium-strength glue is preferable. To use too strong a glue in these circumstances makes it difficult to separate the two halves. Some people recommend a hide glue, Scotch glue, or a hot-melt glue gun for paper bonds.

SIZE OF SURFACE AREA TO BE GLUED

Although the various brands of superglue are strong, they also become very expensive when used over large areas. A cheaper type of glue may be preferred if a lot of it is required. Cascamite or PVA might be more appropriate.

SPEED OF SETTING

If time is of the essence, superglue is undoubtedly the best choice. Some brands also sell accelerators to speed up the setting time even further. It is now also possible to buy epoxy resins that set in a matter of minutes. While not as fast as superglue, or perhaps as convenient, epoxy resin is cheaper if a larger area is to be covered.

MATERIALS TO BE JOINED

If two different materials are to be joined, for example wood and metal, it is necessary to check that the selected glue will actually adhere to both materials. Again, superglue will bond *most* materials, but different brands work better than others in different situations, so it is worth experimenting with several. For example, in my experience, Loctite superglue seems to work better than some others for sticking wire to wood. It is

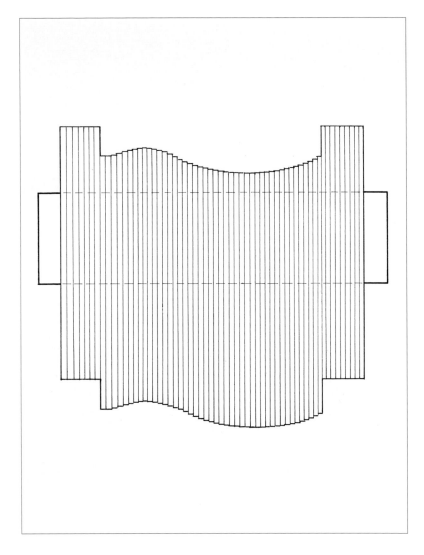

worth mentioning, however, that although superglues may be quite strong, they do not always withstand shocks. While they are quite satisfactory for sticking metal to wood with a bond strong enough to withstand the pressures on the lathe, if the item is dropped onto a hard floor it can sometimes break along the join. For a really strong, shock-resistant bond, an epoxy resin would be more suitable.

GAP-FILLING PROPERTIES

If the two surfaces to be joined are not absolutely flat, there will be some gaps. In these cases a thickish glue will be required to fill them. Cascamite and PVA type glues are fine for this and, similarly, gap-filling (viscous) superglues. Epoxy resin would also be fine.

Fig 2.15 A profile gauge.

3
Timber

■ Sources of scrap wood   ■ Timber features
■ Selection of timber   ■ Sources of timber
■ Suitability of timber

Before making any turned object from wood, the turner must first decide which timber to use. Having decided, the next question is where to get it from as easily and cheaply as possible. If it is a new project – a new technique or an object the turner has never made before – unforeseen problems may arise which can result in the piece being ruined. Therefore it is a good idea to practise on a piece of scrap wood first.

SOURCES OF SCRAP WOOD

Offcuts from ordinary timber merchants will often be quite adequate for experimenting on, be it for trying out a new technique or simply for practising tool control. Many timber merchants are happy to put aside offcuts that would otherwise have been thrown away (an advantage of making small items!). Make sure that you ask for *hardwood* offcuts as anything else will probably be too soft. Many varieties of conifer sold to the building trade or for DIY purposes are too soft for turning. The grain tends to tear unless the tools are extremely sharp and in the hands of a skilled turner. If you ask the timber merchant for hardwood offcuts you are likely to get a selection of different varieties, of varying degrees of quality. Most of it will be quite suitable for practice pieces. (*See* Notes 3.1 and 3.2.)

SELECTION OF TIMBER

After your practice piece has been made you will be in a position to consider the type of timber to use for the item proper. There are so many different varieties of timber to choose from that it can be difficult to know where to start. (*See* Appendix on page 145 for a list of some of the more popular and readily accessible timbers, with a brief description of each.) Some suppliers of specialist timbers produce illustrated charts of all the woods that they stock (often to be found in their catalogues). It can be useful and informative to look at some of these to get an idea of what is available, the variety of colours, grain features, densities, and so forth.

Sometimes one's choice of timber is limited to what is available locally. Some suppliers operate mail order schemes, but the additional costs of postage and packing can often make the prices a little too high. Also, many people prefer to actually *see* what they are buying, particularly when colour is an important consideration. There is often a tremendous variation in colour tone within a single species and it can be disappointing to receive a piece through mail order which is not quite of the colour shade or grain pattern that you had anticipated. Another disadvantage of receiving goods through mail order is that occasionally a piece may be sent that is split. A reputable firm should replace this, but it creates more bother for the turner, especially if the blank is needed at short notice.

By far the best way to purchase turning blanks is to visit a specialist timber supplier that caters for woodturners. They usually have a good range of turning blanks in stock which can be closely inspected before purchase. Unfortunately, such suppliers are few and far between, so many turners have to travel some distance to reach one, and this can limit choice considerably.

Another limitation on one's choice of timber is the cost. Very often the most attractive timbers are also the ones that are the most expensive. However, since most items of jewellery are small, only very small quantities are needed, so even expensive timbers can be purchased without the price being prohibitive. Sometimes specialist timber merchants have an 'offcut box' with small pieces being sold cheaply because they are so small and of little use for most projects. They are often ideal for jewellery.

SUITABILITY OF TIMBER

This is an extremely important consideration because the choice of wood can make an enormous difference to the overall appearance of the finished item of jewellery,

NOTE 3.1 It should be remembered that the term hardwood does not refer to the hardness of the timber. A hardwood is any broad-leaved deciduous tree, and although the timber from such trees does, in general, tend to be hard, there are exceptions to the rule, such as balsa, poplar and some varieties of mahogany. Similarly, the term 'softwood' does not indicate that the wood is literally soft – it refers to the conifers, most of which tend to be fast growing. Again, softwoods do tend to be soft, though there are exceptions, the most notable being yew.

NOTE 3.2 In some cases you may be supplied with pieces of mahogany from endangered sources. Whether you choose to accept this will depend on your viewpoint (*see* page 20). Remember, though, that beggars can't be choosers and if a timber merchant is doing you a favour by putting aside some offcuts, they will not take kindly to being interrogated about its source. Better to decide on your views on this issue before going on the scrounge!

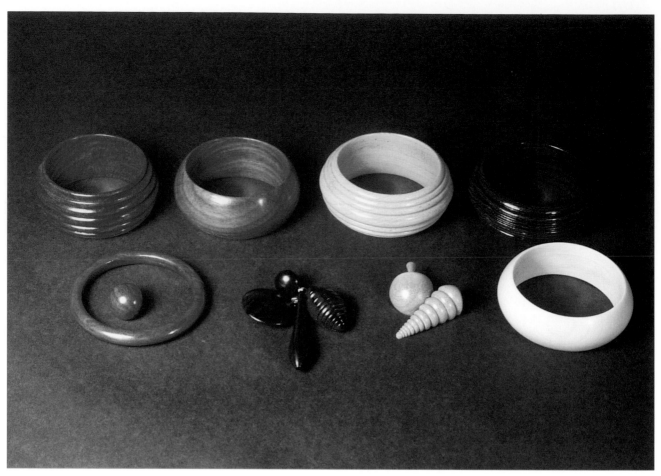

Fig 3.1 Some brightly coloured natural timbers. From left to right: (top row) purple heart, padauk, mupanda, wenge; (bottom row) rosita, violet rosewood, amarello, sycamore.

and it is true to say that some woods are more suitable than others. There are so many factors that need to be considered when choosing timber that it is hard to generalize. However, it would be true to say that, in general, close-grained, dense hardwoods make the most suitable woods for turning jewellery. Coarse-grained timbers are less suitable because the smaller the item the more apparent the grain size becomes and it tends to detract from the shape and form. They also tend to lack the lustre of the fine-grained varieties. Nevertheless, some coarse-grained timbers are fine for larger items such as broad bangles. (Oak is a good example of this because its attractive pattern of rings and rays can be shown to good effect on a bangle.) The dense hardwoods are particularly suitable for jewellery since they tend to take a good polish and have an attractive lustre.

TIMBER FEATURES

Having made these general points, there are other factors that need to be considered before selecting timber:

COLOUR

This is a crucial factor when choosing timber. Jewellery is an important fashion accessory, and when the colours of jewellery and clothing are well matched, the effect can be stunning. Many types of timber are highly attractive and brightly coloured and are ideal for jewellery (*see* Fig 3.1). Purple heart, amarello and rosita are all good examples. Purists might argue that all wood is beautiful and that even the less interesting, dull brown varieties are worthy of conversion into jewellery. While this may in theory be true, the reality is that few people wish to look as if they are wearing a lump of old wood – even if that is exactly what it is! The duller, less obviously attractive varieties of timber can, of course, be decorated by other techniques, such as those mentioned in Chapter 14.

Sometimes you may wish to stain wood to a particular colour that is not available in natural form. Since the staining of timber is such a large issue, Chapter 11 is devoted entirely to it.

(The Appendix on page 145 gives a list of some commonly available timbers, classified according to their colour.)

GRAIN FEATURES

Some timbers have highly attractive grain features such as streaks or stripes of contrasting colours, swirling patterns, colour differences between heartwood and sapwood, interesting knots, and so on. Other timbers are of an even colour throughout. Again, it is important to decide whether the finished item would look better in a uniform colour, or whether it would be enhanced by the grain patterns. This will depend partly on the type of item to be made, its size, and shape. It will also partly depend upon personal preference. If two or more timbers are to be laminated, it is better to choose ones of uniform colour (*see* Chapter 13 for details).

SIZE OF OBJECT TO BE MADE

As mentioned earlier, the larger the item, the more acceptable it is to use a coarse-grained timber. Also, where there is an interesting grain feature, a larger item, such as a broad bangle, will show it off to its best advantage.

SUITABILITY FOR STAINING

This will only be an occasional consideration, since on most occasions, the turner will prefer to use the natural colour. However, there are times when staining is useful, and it is important to be aware that some timbers take a stain more readily than others. For further details on staining, *see* Chapter 11.

DENSITY

The density of a timber is indicated by its specific gravity, which refers to its density in relation to water. The higher the number, the more dense the timber. All but the very densest woods have a specific gravity of less than one (which is why most woods float). As a rule of thumb, the denser the wood, the better the finish is likely to be, though this is not always the case. Dense woods often have a high lustre, a fine grain and take a good polish – all the desirable elements for jewellery. Some suppliers' catalogues indicate the specific gravities of their timbers. In the Appendix on page 145 the specific gravities have been given alongside most of the timbers listed.

As might be expected, most woods with a high density tend to be quite hard, and those with low densities are likely to be soft, though again there are exceptions to this. For example, sycamore, lacewood plane, walnut and cherry are all hard but light, with specific gravities of around 0.5 to 0.6. In spite of their low densities, they are all good turning timbers, and sycamore in particular takes a beautifully smooth finish. (*See* Note 3.3.)

SOURCES OF TIMBER

As mentioned earlier in the chapter, specialist timber merchants usually stock a good range of turning blanks. However, there are other sources which can offer small pieces of wood. Lace bobbin blanks, for example, are ideal for long, thin-stemmed earrings. They come in a wide range of different timber species and are relatively inexpensive, though the price varies according to the species. They can be purchased at lace fairs, at woodworking and woodturning exhibitions, and through mail order. Buying lace bobbin blanks is also a relatively cheap way of sampling a wide variety of timbers with which you may be unfamiliar. Lace bobbin blanks do tend to be very narrow, however, and can be somewhat limiting in that respect.

NOTE 3.3 As mentioned earlier in the chapter, it is important when buying turning blanks to check them over very carefully and to reject any that are split or have other defects. Sometimes a blank will have begun to spalt and this will result in discoloured patches. With some timbers, such as beech, this can produce a very attractive effect. In others it will simply appear smudgy. Unfortunately, if the spalting is only slight it will not necessarily be visible from the outside of the blank, and it may only become apparent as you cut deeper into the wood during the turning process. This is particularly annoying if the spalt only reveals itself towards the finishing stages of cutting. There is nothing you can do about this. If you are determined to save the item in order to justify the amount of time spent on it, spraying it with an opaque pigment can work acceptably (*see* Chapter 14 for details).

Fig 3.2 Earrings made from piano keys.

RECYCLED TIMBER

Second-hand or recycled sources are often the most satisfying to come across, partly because they are cheap (often free) and partly because they will occasionally yield pieces of wood that are otherwise hard to obtain. They can also be of a high quality, as well as being well seasoned. For example, pieces of broken antique furniture can be good sources of mahogany and rosewood. Rubbish skips, attics, car-boot sales, jumble sales, junk shops are all worth investigating in search of such pieces.

A piece of broken chairleg may be useless to most people, but if the timber is suitable and of good quality with no rot or infestation, then with a little skill and imagination it can be converted into several fine pieces of jewellery.

Another good example of recycled wood is old, discarded ebony piano keys. Some piano restorers are happy to sell these quite cheaply since they often strip down old pianos and replace all the keys. They make excellent earrings, and not only is it cheap, but it is a source of ebony which is not contributing to the depletion of rainforests (*see* Fig 3.2).

ECOLOGICAL CONSIDERATIONS

The issues surrounding the extraction of timber from threatened sources are highly complex. Most turners would like to feel that the timber they use comes only from sustainable, properly managed sources, and many would be prepared to travel a little further or pay a little extra in order to be sure of purchasing from an environmentally sound source. Unfortunately it is not as easy as that. At least, not yet.

It is extremely difficult to obtain information regarding timber merchants' sources, and suppliers of timber may claim that their own supplies are from properly managed sources, even if they are not. However, there are timber merchants who are genuinely committed to trading in sustainable timber only, but such suppliers are few and, inevitably, they do not stock the full range of timbers that turners may want, though alternatives may be offered instead.

The current state of affairs makes things very difficult for those individuals who would prefer to buy wood from properly managed sources, but who are unable to gain access to reliable and consistent information. One source is Friends of the Earth who publish much literature on the subject.

There is a dilemma for the individual woodturner who would like to buy a specific species of timber for which there is no comparable alternative, yet knowing that this species is under threat of extinction. This is particularly true for turners wishing to make jewellery, who need to use wood that is dense, fine grained and with the attractive colour properties most frequently found in tropical timbers. It could be argued, perhaps, that buying pieces in very small quantities will not substantially affect the global pattern of deforestation, when compared with the large-scale damage caused through 'slash and burn' practices, or over-logging to supply the building trade. The counter argument, of course, is that any purchase of threatened timber, no matter how small, contributes to the existing problem. In the end, like most things, it seems to come down to a matter of moderation and individual conscience.

CHAPTER

4
Chucking Techniques

■ Four-prong drive centre   ■ Expanding dovetail collet
■ Contracting collet chuck   ■ Wooden faceplate
■ Screw chuck

THERE ARE MANY different chucking techniques available, and most turners have their favourites, so some readers may prefer to use different methods to the ones that I describe. In most instances, there is more than one method that can be used and it is up to the individual to decide which technique suits them best. Much of it will depend on what chucking systems they already have. In this chapter I do not intend to describe all possible methods, but will outline five systems that I find quick and easy to use and that can be used most commonly for small items of jewellery.

When very small items are to be turned, this presents certain problems that do not arise for larger objects. Many of the devices that turners possess, such as commercially produced chucks, are simply too large to hold small diameters. Some firms now manufacture chucks specifically for those people who predominantly turn miniatures, lace bobbins, and so forth. However, like all accessories, these do tend to be expensive,

and before making a purchase it is worth considering whether that particular device is absolutely essential, or whether a simpler method could be used as effectively without the expenditure of cash. (In my experience, some of the commercially produced devices designed for holding small stock are not as easy to use as the advertisements might suggest and, more importantly, they sometimes do not hold the wood sufficiently firmly.)

Although working with small stock can present problems, the basic principles of chucking are the same as for larger items. The five methods described below are those that I tend to use most frequently.

FOUR-PRONG DRIVE CENTRE

This is probably the most familiar method of holding a blank that is to be turned between centres. It is a straightforward method, but extra care must be taken when using small stock because there is a danger of splitting the wood when tapping the drive centre into the end grain, especially where the cross section of the blank is less than ½in (13mm). In order to avoid splitting, it is a good idea to drill a small pilot hole into the centre of the end of the blank to accept the point of the drive centre. Then tap the drive centre *gently* into the end of the blank. (Do not tap the blank onto the drive centre while it is mounted in the headstock as this can cause damage to the lathe bearings.) If the wood is not too dense, this method works well — I often use it for turning 'pendant' earrings.

Miniature four-prong drive centres are also available now and I have found these to be very useful (*see* Chapter 2, Fig 2.8). Special chucks of various designs are available that have been created specifically for holding lace bobbin blanks or other small stock. In my experience these can be problematic because the blank has to be absolutely square if the wood is to be held firmly.

Fig 4.1 A contracting collet chuck.

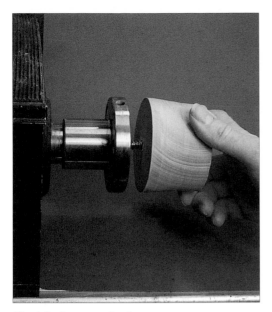

Fig 4.2 A screw chuck.

CONTRACTING COLLET CHUCK

These come in various sizes and can be useful for holding cylinders of wood securely at one end. Contracting collet chucks are useful whenever wood has to be supported without the additional support of a tailstock. The advantage of a contracting collet chuck over a cup chuck is that the diameter of the spigot is not critical since the jaws can close down within a range of diameters. This method could be used for brooches or rings, for example (*see* Chapters 7 and 9). In order for the wood to be held securely, it is important to ensure that the spigot is long enough for the jaws to get a good purchase. Some collet chucks are designed to grip a smaller, dovetailed spigot. The blank must first be roughed down between centres and a spigot of approximately the right diameter is turned at one end. This spigot is then inserted into the contracting collet chuck.

As an alternative to the contracting collet chuck, an ordinary drill chuck can be used on a morse taper which fits into the headstock. This can work well for gripping spigots of a very small diameter. It is a versatile piece of equipment since it can also be used in the tailstock for boring holes.

SCREW CHUCK

This is very useful for turning bangles. A hole corresponding to the size of the screw is drilled in the centre of the blank in the usual way and mounted on the screw chuck in exactly the same manner as one might do when turning a bowl. In this way, a bangle may be half-turned before reverse chucking onto an expanding dovetail collet chuck for finishing the other side (*see* Chapter 8).

EXPANDING DOVETAIL COLLET

These are extremely useful for turning bangles and they save a lot of time. They are a good investment for anyone who plans to turn a lot of bangles. Expanding dovetail collet chucks come in various sizes, including miniature varieties. They grip the wood by expanding into a dovetail recess, for example on the undersides of bowls, but they work equally well on a large parallel recess, such as the inside of a bangle (*see* Chapter 8). The 2½in (64mm) diameter version is ideally suited to bangles (*see* Fig 4.4).

Fig 4.3 An expanding dovetail collet chuck.

Fig 4.4 An expanding dovetail collet chuck, supporting a completed bangle.

WOODEN FACEPLATE

This is probably the simplest and cheapest method of chucking, and one of the most versatile. It has a number of advantages:

▐ It holds the wood at one end very securely indeed without the need for a tailstock (unless the blank is very long and thin).

▐ It can be used for between-centres turning as well as faceplate turning.

▐ There is no need for reverse chucking, e.g. for inserting a turned spigot into a chuck.

▐ There is hardly any wastage of timber, unlike some systems where you have to allow for the length of the spigot which is gripped inside a chuck.

▐ It can be used for tiny scraps that would otherwise be too small to turn (*see* Fig 4.5).

▐ It can be used for irregular-shaped objects such as tagua nuts and pieces of cow horn (*see* Fig 4.6 and Chapter 17).

▐ It is ideal for small stock wood which is very dense and prone to splitting if a four-prong drive is tapped into the end grain.

▐ It does not involve time spent grappling with complicated multipurpose chucks and their associated components.

Fig 4.5 Turning a small bead from a scrap of cow horn glued to the centre of a wooden faceplate.

Fig 4.6 A piece of cow horn glued to the wooden faceplate.

METHOD

1 Select a small metal faceplate. The size is not critical, but if you are turning predominantly small stock using this method it seems logical to use a small faceplate. If the diameter is too large you may find it more difficult to get in really close to the wooden faceplate for shaping and parting off, since its edge will get in the way. This is particularly true if you are working with a very small blank.

2 Screw to the faceplate a piece of circular scrap wood slightly larger in diameter than the faceplate and approximately ¾in (19mm) thick. (These dimensions are not critical and will depend largely on the dimensions of the objects to be turned and the length of your screws.) Make sure that the scrap wood is properly flat on the side to be screwed to the faceplate, in order to ensure stability.

3 With the lathe running, rough down the scrap wood to a cylinder, then true up the end face. Check with a straight edge that this surface is flat with no ridges.

4 With the lathe running, mark a series of concentric rings in pencil on the end face (*see* Fig 4.7). This is not essential but it is enormously helpful as a guide for centring the blank in the middle of the faceplate.

5 Select the blank to be turned and ensure that the end to be glued to the faceplate is flat. This can be done with a bandsaw or belt sander.

6 Using cyanoacrylate glue, stick the blank to the centre of the faceplate using the concentric rings as a guide. If time is short, cyanoacrylate accelerator can be used to speed up the setting time. This will enable you to turn the blank straight away.

7 If you are turning a long, thin blank, e.g. for a thin-stemmed earring, bring up the tailstock in the usual fashion to provide additional support.

8 When the item has been finished and parted off you will be left with the remains of the blank still glued firmly to the centre of the faceplate. This can be sliced off using a skew chisel, with the lathe running.

9 True up the faceplate with a skew chisel once again ready for the next blank.

In this way, the same faceplate can be used over and over. Remember, though, that with successive 'true ups' with the skew chisel, the wooden faceplate will very gradually get thinner. It is worth remembering the length of the screws that you have used to fix it to the metal faceplate, otherwise you will run the risk of damaging your skew on a protruding screw!

See Note 4.1.

NOTE 4.1 Although a faceplate is used in this method, it is important to understand that it is only being used as a general means of supporting the wood. It is not necessarily being used for what is often referred to as faceplate turning, where the grain is running at right angles to the bed bars. Although it may indeed be used in precisely this fashion, it may also be used (as described above) for spindle or between- centres turning where the grain is running parallel to the bed bars. In these instances, the faceplate is simply being used as an alternative to a four-prong drive, a collet chuck, or similar.

Fig 4.7 Concentric rings marked on the wooden faceplate to act as a centring guide.

CHAPTER

5
Design

█ Form
█ Function
█ Proportion
█ Inspiration from nature

█ Repetition
█ Balance
█ Delicacy
█ Summary

A GROUP OF SIMILAR objects, individually designed, will always possess differing degrees of visual appeal. Some will receive widespread acclaim, while others will not attract a second look. Why? A successful designer (be they architect, fashion designer, engineer, or jewellery designer) will usually have some understanding of why some objects are generally accepted as being more attractive than others of a similar nature. If we can understand why some things work visually and others do not, it will give us an advantage when it comes to designing jewellery. Of course, there is always a measure of subjectivity here, and often widespread disagreement about a particular design. That is why there can never be any absolute rules. It would be very boring if everyone liked the same things. Nevertheless, it is sometimes possible to identify objects whose designs do have wide general appeal, and which are accepted by a fairly large majority as being 'good'.

So what constitutes 'good' design? The overall appearance of any object is determined by a combination of factors: shape, colour, texture, size etc. In this chapter, however, I am going to concentrate largely on 'form', since this is rather an elusive quality, yet such a vital one.

FORM

What is meant by 'form'? According to Frank E. Cummings*, 'form is three-dimensional and, in general, it can only be perceived when light strikes it from the side. Form usually includes all the surface characteristics of the object. In the case of a woodturned object, we are perceiving grain, value, texture and colour.'

Shape, on the other hand, is a two-dimensional concept, and is created by the *lines* of the object. The *line* refers to the actual shape of a given edge, be it straight, tightly curved, or smoothly flowing. This is a highly significant element in design and is one of the characteristics that determine appeal. Good bowl designs, for example, often have well-defined, strong, sweeping curves. But this alone is not enough. Sweeping curves are all very well, but where should they begin and end? How tightly curved should they be? Where should the widest point be? These are all matters concerned with proportion (*see* page 28).

Shape and form are crucial elements. Very often, particularly in the field of woodturning, one sees an object, perhaps a bowl or a vase, that reveals a high level of advanced skill, yet sadly its awkward and cumbersome shape lets it down badly. It seems fundamental, therefore, that shape and form should be an early consideration in the planning stage of any object.

Although there are no rules when it comes to designing an object, there *are* limitations imposed by the intended function of that object. According to the Bauhaus philosophy, 'form follows function'. In other words, the function must be our primary consideration.

FUNCTION

Jewellery is designed to be worn comfortably and easily. That must be the starting point. If it is not comfortable, if it gets in the way, if it gets entangled in clothing, it will not be worn. This is one of the primary considerations when designing any piece of jewellery. But the main purpose of jewellery is decoration of the human body, and so jewellery must also be attractive. Therefore the task of the jewellery designer is to create jewellery that is appealing and that compliments the wearer, while at the same time remaining within the boundaries of practicality.

Sometimes the intention is to create jewellery that is eye-catching; sometimes it is to create jewellery that makes a statement about the wearer. At other times jewellery is required to be discreet and to offset an outfit

American Woodturner, December 1991, Vol.6, No.4; and *Woodturning* magazine Nov/Dec 1992, Issue 11.

of clothing. Whatever the purpose, the designer must ensure that the shape and form conform to the practical requirements. For example, when making long, thin-stemmed earrings, it is easy to get carried away and end up with an incredibly long and fine pair of earrings, with perhaps beautiful shape and form, which could, at first glance, appear to be a masterpiece of turning design. However, if it then transpires that they cannot be worn by anyone unless they have an abnormally long neck, their purpose has been defeated. The length of a pair of earrings, then, will be dictated by a number of considerations: the personal preference of the wearer, the length of their neck, and whether they intend to wear them with high, roll-necked collars, which would interfere with their drop. Another consideration would be whether they are intended for everyday wear or occasional evening wear.

Similarly, an item of jewellery may be large, but it must not be too heavy. A brooch would sag and a bangle would become uncomfortable if they weighed too much. Since the weight of an object depends partly upon its density, the type of wood used is something that should be taken into account at the design stage. The density of wood can vary quite a lot (*see* Appendix on page 145), although by and large it tends to be a fairly light substance in comparison with, say, metal. Function, then, may be

thought of as a framework within which we may create the form.

PROPORTION

To quote Frank E. Cummings★ again: 'Proportion refers to the relative comparison between one part or element of a form and another. For example, the height of a turned form might be compared with its width. The size of the top of a turned vessel might be compared with the size of its base.'

The proportions of an object are another key element in design success. Usually, a good designer knows when something looks right. Others find it harder to judge. Some designers refer to a mathematical principle of proportion called the golden mean (also known as the golden section or golden ratio).

THE GOLDEN MEAN
This formula is based on the ratio of 1:1.618, and was first noticed by Euclid around 300 BC. Its most well-known application is in the construction of the golden rectangle, whose sides have relative lengths in the ratio 1:1.618 (*see* Fig 5.1). Such rectangles are widely thought to have particularly pleasing proportions and several experiments have revealed that this particular rectangular shape is highly popular. For this reason, many picture frames are constructed along these lines. Architects sometimes carry this further and construct houses whose windows conform to this ratio. Indeed, the architect Le Corbusier used the golden ratio extensively within his designs.

Even more interesting is the fact that this ratio occurs time and time again in nature. Spirals, such as the type found in nautilus shells, for example, are constructed from combinations of golden rectangles (*see* Fig 5.2). Another example is the spiral formation of the seeds within a fir cone or a pineapple.

★*American Woodturner*, December 1991, Vol.6, No.4; and *Woodturning* magazine Nov/Dec 1992, Issue 11.

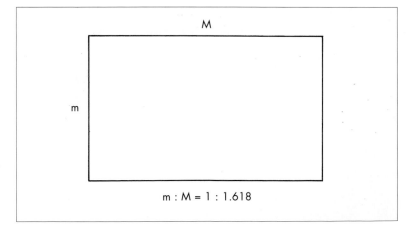

Fig 5.1 The golden rectangle.

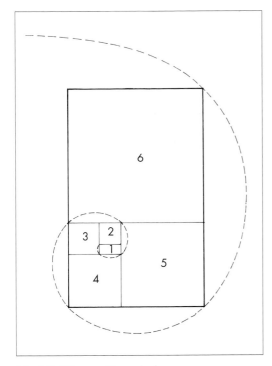

Fig 5.2 The nautilus spiral.

Many plants, in fact, have their flowers and petals arranged according to the golden ratio. No wonder it is thought to have such significance within the world of design. But how might it be applied to jewellery? There are some possibilities. For example, within a given golden rectangle, we could draw a variety of shapes that correspond to the golden ratio and that could be used in jewellery design (*see* Figs 5.3 and 5.4). Further experimentation could produce other variations.

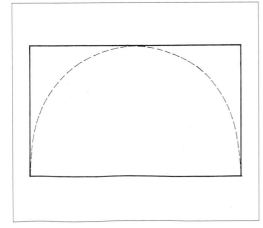

Fig 5.3 A cross section through a broad bangle, based on the golden rectangle.

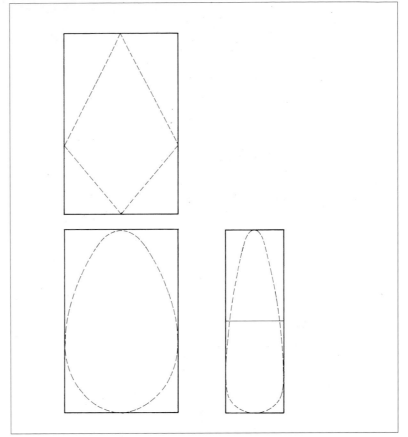

Fig 5.4 Possibilities for earring design based on the golden rectangle.

INSPIRATION FROM NATURE

Despite the significance and attraction of the golden mean, to confine oneself within its limits would be contrived and constricting, as well as unnecessary. Nevertheless, the notion of looking to nature for designs is a good one, and this was a practice that was widely adopted by the Art Nouveau movement around the turn of the century. Animals, birds, plants, insects, shells – all were used for inspiration, and these stylized representations were integral to the basic shapes and forms. According to Art Nouveau designer Henry Van de Velde, 'Ornament and the form should appear so intimate that the ornament seems to have determined the form.' And according to William Hardy, 'The essence of Art Nouveau is a line, a sinuous extended curve... Art Nouveau rejected the order of the straight line.'*

★A Guide to Art Nouveau Style William Hardy (Quintet, 1987).

Within the realms of woodturning it can be hard to emulate the detailed forms reminiscent of Art Nouveau unless it is combined with carving. Nevertheless there are some possibilities. Figs 5.5 and 5.6 show two brooches whose shapes resemble the segmented nature of some natural forms. There are a number of possible variations on this theme.

NATURE HAS NO STRAIGHT LINES

The rejection of straight lines, referred to above, is a principle worthy of consideration by the woodturner, since woodturners are primarily concerned with producing curves. There are exceptions to this, of course, where a straight line is needed or desired, but by and large the curve is the predominant line. One of the commonest pitfalls for the novice turner is producing a curved line that contains a flat area somewhere along its length. This may not at first be apparent, and the turner may wonder why the shape does not look quite right. Eventually the error will be spotted. It is so easy to produce flats within a curve that it is worth making a conscious effort, when turning, to avoid them. Fig 5.7 illustrates how a flat can mar the appearance of a bangle. Fig 5.8 shows a similar effect on an earring. In other words, within a curve there should be a 'continuity of line' with no sudden changes of direction.

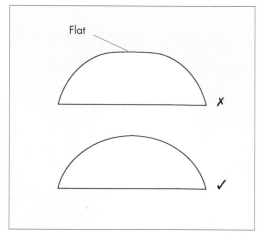

Fig 5.7 The cross sections of two bangles. Avoid flat areas on the curves.

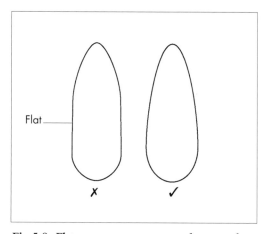

Fig 5.8 Flat areas on curves can also mar the appearance of earrings.

So far we have considered some basic principles concerning the elements of function, form, line and proportion. There are, however, other elements that are worth examining:

REPETITION

Within any form, there is a possibility for repetition, either in terms of some decorative feature – such as beads or inlaid lines – or in terms of shape. Such repetition can often be used to advantage. Fig 5.9 shows a pair of earrings where the curve at the base is repeated (or echoed) by the curves of the silver lines. If the curves had differed, the design would not have worked so well. This is also illustrated in Fig 5.10.

Fig 5.5 A segmented brooch made from amarello, whose shape resembles a shell.

Fig 5.6 A segmented brooch made from rosewood, whose shape resembles a chrysalis.

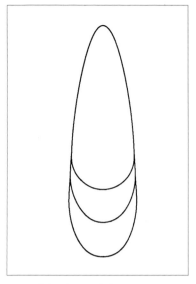

Fig 5.9   **Figs 5.9 and 5.10 The curve of the base of the**   Fig 5.10
earrings is echoed in the curves of the silver lines.

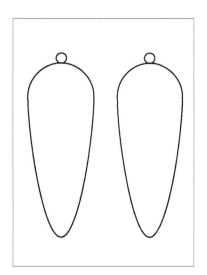

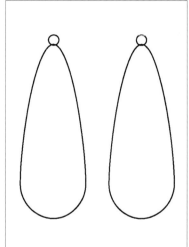

Fig 5.11 An unbalanced orientation.   **Fig 5.12 A balanced orientation.**

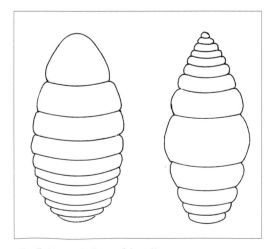

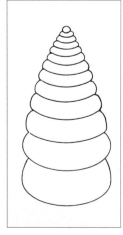

Fig 5.13 Unbalanced beading.   **Fig 5.14 Balanced beading.**

BALANCE

Every design should have balance. This can refer to physical aspects, as in Figs 5.11 and 5.12. The earrings in both pictures are exactly the same. The only difference is their orientation. There is no reason why they should not be suspended as they are in Fig 5.11, except that they look unbalanced – probably because their position is an unstable one. In Fig 5.12 the position is altogether more stable and looks more balanced.

Balance can also refer to more integral aspects of design. For example, Fig 5.13, shows an unbalanced use of beading. Fig 5.14 shows a more pleasing arrangement.

DELICACY

It is important not to confuse 'delicate' with 'small'. Most items of jewellery tend to be small, but that does not mean to say that they are necessary delicate. Equally, if a piece of jewellery does happen to be on the large side, that does not necessarily mean that it is heavy and clumsy. Some of the most beautiful examples of Roman and Celtic jewellery, for example, are very large, but they also have an exquisite delicacy.

Wooden jewellery, in particular, has a tendency to look clumsy, so special care must be taken to prevent this. Unlike metal, it cannot be beaten, cast, or rolled into delicate filaments or thin sheets. The very structure of wood dictates that it must remain in a fairly substantial lump. The skill of the turner, therefore, is directed towards rendering the wooden item as 'un-lumplike' as possible, while retaining its strength and rigidity. To a certain extent, knowledge of the relative properties – density, grain length, etc. – of different species of wood can help. Some woods, such as ebony, can be worked more finely than others.

However, there are other factors at work here and delicacy is inevitably linked to line and shape. We are all familiar with optical illusions; for example, straight lines that look curved and curved lines that look straight. Depth of field, perspective, relative size, distance – all these things are susceptible to distortion through our own perceptions. In other words, the eye is easily deceived. This is a useful piece of knowledge for designers. Architects have known for centuries that cathedral spires, if built truly straight, can appear as if they have a bulge in the middle. To avoid this effect they were often built with slightly concave sides, giving the appearance of straight lines (*see* Fig 5.15).

In woodturning, there is often a necessity to exaggerate curves in order to achieve an intended shape. For example, a narrow neck needs to be made narrower than one might think, otherwise it will look too wide. An outwardly sweeping curve needs to sweep out even more dramatically than one might expect in order to achieve the desired impact. A thin stem needs to be made even thinner, and so forth. This latter point is particularly important when making long-stemmed earrings – stems that are too thick can contribute to an overall lack of delicacy.

Finally, there are a couple of tips that readers may find useful:

1 With small objects, such as jewellery, any surface defect will show up easily. It is particularly important, therefore, that the lines of the object are completely smooth and free from any slight ridges. It is worth remembering that, even with a good light, the eye cannot detect imperfections in the surface as well as the finger can. A surface that looks smooth may actually have ridges on it. By running the fingers gently along the surface these will soon be felt.

2 During the final stages of turning, very light cuts are made to perfect the final lines. In order to be able to see the shape clearly, it is a good idea to place on the lathe bed a sheet of paper of a contrasting colour to the object. This enables the profile of the object to be more clearly discerned.

SUMMARY

Although opinion may be divided on the relative merits of some designs, there are others that attract almost universal appeal. Why is it that some designs are so successful? What is it that the others lack? The answers to these questions are elusive, and subliminal perception (of which little is understood) may play a significant part. Nevertheless, it is possible to analyse some aspects of design that can bring us a little nearer to our goal. There are no hard and fast rules, but there are some general principles that can help us to achieve better results.

Consideration of elements such as form, function, shape and line can focus our attention on those aspects of design that contribute to general appeal. Balance, repetition of line, and delicacy can also sometimes enhance the appearance of an object.

Continuity (of curves) is essential and nature can often provide us with some unusual inspiration.

As the novice turner becomes more experienced, they will become more used to looking at shapes and will become more aware of design features in general. It is useful to study different shapes, memorizing the good ones, while trying to decide why others are less appealing.

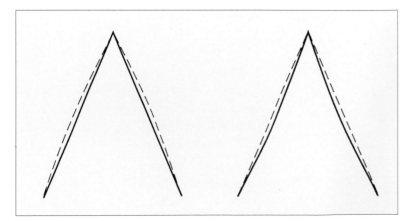

Fig 5.15 The 'church spire' effect. The continuous lines represent the real shape, while the dotted lines represent the perceived shape, which is an optical illusion.

PART TWO
Projects

Earrings

Brooches

Bangles

Rings

Necklaces

6

Earrings

▌ Pendant earrings   ▌ Some variations
▌ Stud earrings   ▌ Decorative techniques

LEVEL OF SKILL: Novice to intermediate

LTHOUGH EARRINGS come in all shapes and sizes, there are two fundamental designs from which they all originate. The first is the type that is suspended from the earlobe and hangs freely from a wire. The shape and length can vary (*see* Fig 6.1) according to personal taste. (For details on design and form, *see* Chapter 5.) The second

design is a shape that is flat on one side (the back) and is attached directly to the earlobe by means of a thin stud and an earpost and scroll (*see* Fig 6.2).

The first type of earring looked at in this chapter is the suspended form, referred to as the pendant earring. When turned on the lathe these may often take the approximate shape of a teardrop. This can be long and thin, or short and fat; it can have a blunt end or a pointed end; it can have straight or sloping sides; it can be angular or smooth. Fig 6.4 illustrates a variety of possibilities for the basic pendant design.

Fig 6.1 Suspended earrings can vary in size and shape.

Fig 6.2 Stud earrings are attached to the ear by means of an earpost and scroll.

Fig 6.3 A collection of stud earrings. Clockwise from the left: Brazilian purple heart, violet rosewood, violet rosewood, rosita.

Fig 6.4 A variety of designs for pendant earrings.

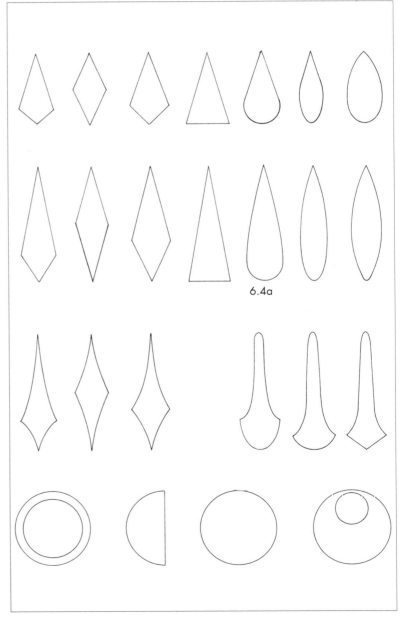

6.4a

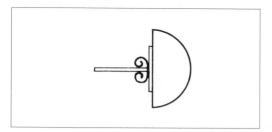

Fig 6.5 A stud earring.

The second type of design – which fastens directly onto the earlobe – takes the form of a hemisphere when turned on the lathe. This form is known as a stud earring (*see* Fig 6.5). Here, there is less scope for variation in terms of shape than with the pendant variety, but variation can be introduced through other means, such as size, colour and texture.

Sometimes these two basic designs are combined in one, where a stud earring has a pendant suspended from it (*see* Fig 6.6). This chapter describes the techniques for producing both of the basic designs.

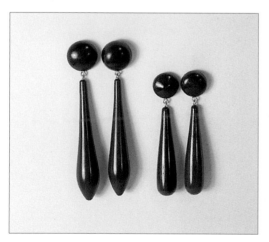

Fig 6.6 Rosewood earrings incorporating both 'drop' and 'stud' designs.

PENDANT EARRINGS

1 Select a small piece of timber with the grain running lengthwise, preferably a dense, fine-grained timber, e.g. purple heart (*see* Chapter 3). Bandsaw the selected piece to a blank of the required dimensions. The precise measurements will obviously depend upon the final desired dimensions of the item, but the following measurements of the blank would give an earring of medium size:

Length: 3⅛in (79mm) – this allows for some wastage at either end.

Width: ¾in (19mm)

2 Drill a small hole in the centre of one end to accept the centre pin of the four-prong drive. Do not attempt to hammer the drive centre into the endgrain, or it will split the wood. *Lightly* tap the drive centre into the end of the blank, mount the blank on the lathe, and bring up the tailstock in the usual way. (*See* Note 6.1.)

3 Rough down the blank to a cylinder in the usual way.

4 It is now necessary to decide upon the desired size and shape for the earring. Fig 6.4 shows some examples.

The following instructions describe the creation of a pair of earrings 2⅛in (54mm) long and ½in (13mm) at the widest point, of a design illustrated in Fig 6.4a. However, the same techniques and principles would apply to pendant earrings of any size and shape.

Now begin the shaping, remembering always to work 'downhill'. A skew chisel is ideal for this procedure but a thin bowl gouge (*see* Fig 6.7) or a spindle gouge can be used effectively. Remember also to leave approximately ⅜in (10mm) at either end to enable you to part off easily.

NOTE 6.1 It is extremely useful to have a miniature drive centre for thin blanks such as these, but it is by no means essential (*see* page 12). An ordinary four-prong drive will do the job unless the blank is very thin. An alternative means of chucking the blank is in a morse taper drill chuck mounted in the headstock, or a four-jaw contracting chuck, if you have one. However, both these latter methods require a fair amount of excess wood to be embedded in the chuck. If you want to make maximum use of the length of your blank, with minimum wastage, it is better to mount it between centres using an ordinary drive centre or a wooden faceplate as described in Chapter 4. One advantage of using a drill chuck or a four-jaw contracting chuck, however, is that one end of the blank remains free, enabling you to finish that end completely before parting off. However, if the blank is very long and thin, there may be insufficient support without the use of the tailstock, and this can result in excessive vibration.

Fig 6.7 A thin bowl gouge in use. Remember to always cut 'downhill'.

NOTE 6.2 You may
also find that miniature
turning tools are helpful
on small items such as
earrings, but they are
by no means essential.
All the required cutting
can
be carried out with
standard turning tools
of a medium size. A
¾in (20mm) roughing
gouge and a ⅜in
(10mm) bowl gouge
are quite satisfactory.

5 As the diameter of the blank becomes
smaller, it will be necessary to bring the tool
rest nearer to the work. It may be difficult to
do this if you are using a long tool rest,
because there will be insufficient room
between the headstock and tailstock. This is
where a very short tool rest is useful (*see* page
11). Even a standard short 5in (127mm) rest
will be too long, so if you are able to make
your own or get one made to your own
specifications, it is well worth it. I find that a
2½in (64mm) tool rest is ideal for earrings.
(*See* Note 6.2.)

6 Continue cutting slowly and carefully,
keeping in mind the considerations of shape
and form dictated by the desired dimensions.
In this example, allowing a wastage of ⅜in
(10mm) at either end, shape the work so that

the outline of the earring is clearly delineated
(*see* Fig 6.8). Continue to cut until the final
desired dimensions have been reached.

7 At this stage, certain forms of decoration
may be added; scorch rings, for example (*see*
Chapter 14). Sand and finish.

8 Finally, continue to remove the
remaining pieces of wood at either end until
the earring is supported only by very thin
spigots (*see* Figs 6.8 and 6.9). You may now
want to do some further sanding at the ends
and to apply finish to the sections that have
been revealed by further cutting. Indeed, you
may wish to repeat this process, paring away
more and more at the ends until you feel
that you can remove no more without
parting off. The earring may now be
supported by spigots as thin as ¹⁄₁₆in (1½mm).
The size of the spigots will depend partly
upon the density of the timber. A very dense
timber, such as ebony, will support the work
on very fine spigots, whereas a less dense
timber would require slightly thicker spigots.

9 Part off carefully from one end. A thin
skew chisel is ideal for this, but it is quite
acceptable to use whatever method and
whatever tools you find easiest. Sometimes it
is easier and safer to remove the waste from
one end using a mini-hacksaw, but it is
important to do this with the lathe switched
off and by rotating the spindle slowly by hand
as you gently saw through.

10 Saw away the remaining waste wood
from the opposite end. Sand and finish the
extreme ends by hand.

11 Now comes the difficult bit. Repeat
the whole procedure for the second earring,
trying to match the first one as closely as
possible. This can take quite a while because
it is necessary to keep stopping the lathe to
compare with the finished earring. If you are
not sufficiently confident to match by eye, it
is a good idea to use a pair of callipers,

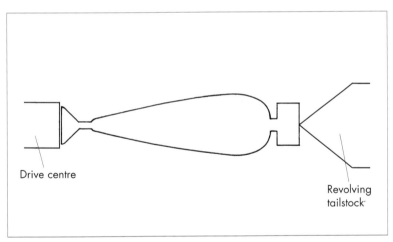

Drive centre

Revolving
tailstock

Fig 6.8

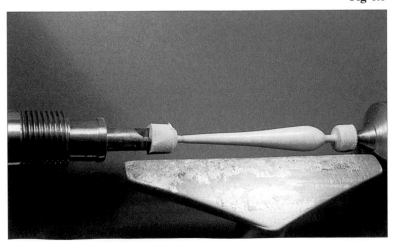

**Figs 6.8 and 6.9 Continue to cut until the earring is
supported only by a very thin spigot at each end.**

Fig 6.9

Fig 6.10 Drill the hole vertically.

The size of the drill bit is also critical. The size of the hole must correspond to the thickness of the eyelet wire that will be inserted. (The size of the drill bit and the thickness of the eyelet wire may be partly determined by what is available to you in your area. Very fine drill bits can be hard to acquire even from specialist tool merchants.) You should aim to drill a hole that is no more than ½sin (1mm) in diameter. The eyelet wire should slip into the hole comfortably but without too much gap.

You will also need a pin vice to accept this drill bit since it is too small to be gripped in a normal drill chuck (*see* page 13). Make sure that your pin vice is of the smallest possible size – the jaws should close down completely. These items can be found at specialist tool merchants. (*See* Note 6.3.)

13 When the holes have been drilled, insert an eyelet wire (*see* Fig 6.11) and glue in place with superglue.

14 When the glue has dried, attach an 'ear-wire' to each eyelet (*see* Figs 6.12 and 6.13). (For more details of jewellery findings, *see* Chapter 16.)

For advice on turning thin, long-stemmed earrings, *see* Note 6.4.

NOTE 6.3 When securing small items such as earrings in a vice prior to drilling, it is advisable to glue a strip of rubber to the inside edge of each jaw of the vice. This will prevent the metal of the jaws from biting into the wood and leaving a mark.

measuring the width at various points along the length. Another technique would be to cut out from card a template of the first earring, and then regularly check the shaping of the second earring against this. The hardest part is often matching the shape at the bottom end of the earrings. It is very common to find that you have made the second one a little too blunt or too pointed. However, do not worry if the two do not *exactly* match, because when they are being worn, there is always the width of a head in between the two which makes it impossible to observe both in any detail simultaneously! Also, one could argue that part of the charm of handmade items is their slight irregularities, which distinguish them from mass-produced objects.

12 Drill a small hole vertically in the end of each stem (*see* Fig 6.10). Although it is possible to do this by hand with an ordinary electric drill, it is very difficult unless you have an extremely steady hand, and I would strongly recommend the use of a pillar drill (*see* page 10).

Fig 6.11 Insert an eyelet wire into the drilled hole.

Fig 6.12 Attach the ear wire to the eyelet.

38

NOTE 6.4 If very thin, long-stemmed earrings are required, there are a few extra considerations: first of all, make sure that the wood chosen is suitable. It should ideally be hard and dense with a fine grain. Secondly, it is important to ensure that the tools are extremely sharp at all times. If they are slightly blunt, there will be a tendency for the wood to be pushed off centre, resulting in vibration. For the same reason, take only very fine cuts. Never try to rush the job. Take it slowly and carefully at all times. As the stem gets thinner, you may wish to support it with your fingers to minimize the vibration (*see* Fig 6.14). However, if your experience of turning is limited, you may not feel sufficiently confident to do so at this stage, in which case continue to cut as lightly as possible.

It is worth experimenting with different tools. You may, for example, find that taking light, scraping cuts with a small spindle gouge is more successful than using a cutting action with a bowl gouge or skew chisel. There are really no rules here, except to be mindful of safety.

Fig 6.13 The earring with eyelet and ear wire attached.

Fig 6.14 Support the thin stem with the fingers if possible.

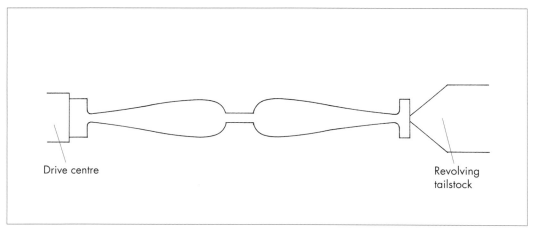

Drive centre

Revolving tailstock

Fig 6.15

Figs 6.15 and 6.16 Turning two earrings from a single blank.

Fig 6.16

ALTERNATIVE METHOD

The method outlined above suggests that each earring needs to be turned separately. While this is true for the thin, long-stemmed variety, it is not necessary for shorter, wider designs. Instead, you may prefer to turn both earrings from a single blank. However, it is wise to ensure that the thinnest parts of the earrings (i.e. the tops) are nearest to the headstock and tailstock, and not in the middle (*see* Figs 6.15 and 6.16). To have the thinnest parts in the middle would weaken the structure and give rise to the aforementioned problems of vibration. Also, try to leave plenty of space between the two ends in the middle. It is very easy to underestimate the amount of space required for parting off. A comfortable distance between the ends of the two earrings would be ½in (50mm). Again, parting off at this point is easiest and safest with a mini-hacksaw, with the lathe stationary.

The advantage of turning both earrings from a single blank is that it is quicker, with only one blank needing to be mounted on the lathe and roughed down. It is also less wasteful of wood. However, there are disadvantages: it is more difficult to ensure that the two pieces are identical because it is not possible to hold one up against the other. Consequently, comparison has to be done by measurement with callipers at each stage, or else by means of a card template.

STUD EARRINGS

There are two methods of producing stud earrings, one with end grain, the other with side grain. Each of these will be described in turn.

END-GRAIN STUDS

1 Decide upon the desired diameter of the finished stud. This can vary enormously but in most cases will probably lie somewhere between ⅜in (10mm) for very small ones and 1³⁄₁₆in (30mm) for very large. The following instructions describe the creation of a pair of earrings of the following dimensions:

Diameter: ¾in (19mm)
Depth: ⁷⁄₁₆in (11mm)

2 Select a suitable piece of timber, preferably fine grained (e.g. sycamore or purple heart) with a square cross section slightly larger than the desired diameter, and long enough to give the depth of two earrings plus some extra for inserting into the chuck. (The depth is the distance between the centre front and the centre back.) Remember also to allow some length for parting off. For this particular example, a blank of the following dimensions is suggested:

Length: 2in (50mm)
Width: 1in (25mm)

3 Mount on the lathe between centres and rough down to a cylinder.

4 Turn a spigot at one end, of the correct diameter to fit into a contracting collet chuck, a cup chuck, a drill chuck or any similar device that holds the wood at one end.

5 Remount the wood in the chuck, and bring the tool rest up parallel with the end grain.

6 Using a bowl gouge, gradually cut away at the corner until a smooth curve is achieved from the centre of the end face to the side face (*see* Figs 6.17 and 6.18).

7 Having thus rounded the end grain, the desired shape of the earring should have been roughly achieved. Check to see if the shape of the dome looks right. Sometimes a shallower curve is desired; sometimes a more hemispherical shape. It all depends on personal taste. Make any final adjustments to the dome until you are fully satisfied with the shape.

In this example, the depth of the hemisphere should be ⁷⁄₁₆in (11mm) and the diameter ⅞in (22mm).

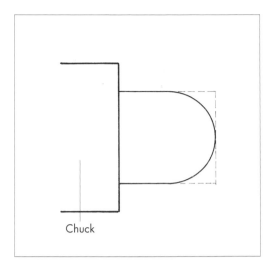

Chuck

Fig 6.17

11 Repeat this procedure with the remainder of the blank, trying to ensure that the second earring matches the first as closely as possible.

12 Having completed both earrings, glue metal earposts and scrolls to the centre of the back of each one (*see* Chapter 16 for details of jewellery findings).

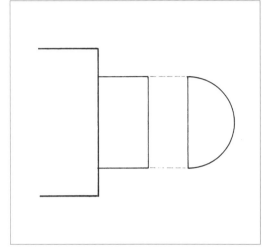

Fig 6.19

Figs 6.17 and 6.18 Round off the **Fig 6.18**
corners to produce a continuous curve
from the centre of the end face to the side face.

8 Sand and finish in the usual way.

9 Bring the tool rest around so that it is once again parallel to the axis. Part off at the desired depth (*see* Figs 6.19 and 6.20). Once again, parting off can be done either with a parting tool or a mini-hacksaw with the lathe being slowly turned by hand (*see* page 37).

10 Sand the back of the earring by hand until it is perfectly smooth, and apply a finish.

Figs 6.19 and 6.20 Part off at the desired depth. **Fig 6.20**

SIDE-GRAIN STUDS

In the case of side-grain studs (unlike the procedure for end-grain), both earrings are turned simultaneously from a blank that has been sawn in half and reassembled using glue and paper.

1 Select a suitable blank (preferably of dense, fine-grained timber) of the following dimensions:

Length: 2¼in (57mm) – this allows sufficient length for insertion into the chuck.
Width: 1in (25mm).

These measurements will give finished earrings of ¾in (19mm) diameter and ⅜in (10mm) depth.

2 Using a bandsaw, saw the blank in half lengthwise.

3 Glue each half back together with a layer of thick paper in between. Do not use too strong a glue, or you may have difficulty in separating the two halves after turning. An impact adhesive, for example, would be suitable. Leave to dry.

4 When the glue has dried, mount the blank on the lathe between centres and rough down to a cylinder.

5 Turn a spigot at one end the correct size for insertion into your chuck.

6 Remount the blank in the chuck.

7 Turn a complete sphere at the end, leaving it attached to the remainder of the blank by a small spigot (*see* Figs 6.21 and 6.22).

8 Make sure that the shape is as near spherical as possible. Make any final adjustments as necessary.

9 Sand, finish and part off.

10 Separate the two halves. This can sometimes be difficult, especially if you have used a glue that is too strong. A sharpened screwdriver inserted between the two halves might be effective.

11 Sand and finish the back of each stud.

12 Attach metal earposts and scrolls (*see* Chapter 16).

See Note 6.5.

NOTE 6.5 The advantage of the side-grain method is that both earrings are bound to be identical since they are turned simultaneously. Another advantage of using this method is that you do not have to turn earrings that are spherical. You can turn any shape you like. Always remember, though, that the end product should be attractive and practical.

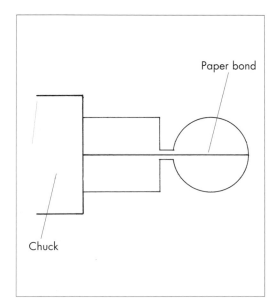

Fig 6.21   Figs 6.21 and 6.22 **Turn a complete sphere, leaving it attached by a single spigot.**   Fig 6.22

Fig 6.23 Pendant earrings in the form of squat cones (purple heart).

SOME VARIATIONS

The earrings shown in Fig 6.23 are essentially of the pendant variety because they are designed to be suspended below the ear. However, they were made by the method described for end-grain studs, the only difference being the size and shape (*see* Fig 6.24). Fig 6.25 shows violet rosewood earrings in the shape of discs, which are similar in design to the 'cones' and were made by the same method (*see* Fig 6.26). A skew chisel was the main tool used for both of the above designs.

Fig 6.24 A 'cone' being turned from end-grain purple heart.

Fig 6.25 'Disc' earrings made from violet rosewood.

Fig 6.26 Turning the disc earrings.

The hoop-shaped earrings in Fig 6.27 were made according to the method for hoop rings described on pages 63–66. Looking at these photos, as well as Figs 6.28 and 6.29, it can be seen that, with a little imagination, limitless variations on a few basic themes can be produced. A particularly pleasing effect can be created by matching brooch and earrings (*see* Chapter 7 for ideas on brooch design).

DECORATIVE TECHNIQUES

There are numerous methods for decorating earrings to make them look more interesting. Examples include inlaying wire (*see* Chapter l2), staining and dyeing (*see* Chapter 11), beading, scorch rings, and the use of metallic pastes and paints (*see* Chapter 14). These, together with the wide variety of sizes, shapes and colours, mean that no two pairs need ever be the same. It is important to remember, though, that too much decoration can spoil the overall appearance. Shape and form should be primary considerations, and decoration should be used sparingly, and only if it will enhance the overall effect (*see* Chapter 5 for further details).

Fig 6.27 'Hoop' earrings turned from end-grain purple heart.

Fig 6.28 African blackwood earrings made from a single turned disc, sawn in half. Haematite beads were glued into pre-drilled holes in the side faces for decoration.

Fig 6.29 Earrings made from turned wooden beads. (For details on bead making, *see* Chapter 10.)

CHAPTER

7
Brooches

▌ End-grain brooch   ▌ Decorative techniques
▌ Side-grain brooch

ESSENTIAL EQUIPMENT

▌ Lathe
▌ Basic turning tools
▌ Contracting collet chuck
   (or similar device)

RECOMMENDED EQUIPMENT

▌ Pillar drill
▌ Band saw

LEVEL OF SKILL: Novice

Brooches can come in all sizes, shapes and forms. In this chapter we will be looking at two basic techniques for making brooches, from which it is possible to produce countless variations. The first is for producing a brooch from end grain; the second, from side grain.

END-GRAIN BROOCH

All brooches made using this method are circular.

1 Select a suitable piece of timber, preferably dense, fine grained, and of the desired colour. The dimensions of the blank will be determined by the chosen dimensions of the finished item. These instructions describe the creation of a brooch of the following dimensions:

Diameter: 1in (25mm)
Depth: ⅝in (16mm)

The width (or cross section) of the blank needs to be slightly larger than the diameter of the finished brooch. The length of the blank should be equal to the depth of the brooch plus some extra for insertion into the chuck (remembering to add on some for parting-off space). For a brooch of the above-stated dimensions, a suitable blank would be of the following size:

Length: 2in (50mm)
Width: 1¼in (32mm)

2 Mount the blank on the lathe between centres with the grain running parallel to the axis.

3 Rough down to a cylinder and turn a spigot at one end of the correct size to fit the chuck.

4 Remount the blank in the chuck, and bring the tool rest around so that it is facing the end grain.

5 Using a bowl gouge, gradually cut away the corner edge to produce a sweeping curve from the centre of the end face to the side face (*see* Figs 7.1 and 7.2).

6 Examine the dome shape thus produced. Is it the shape you want? Some curves can be very shallow, while others are more hemispherical. Try to ensure that you have

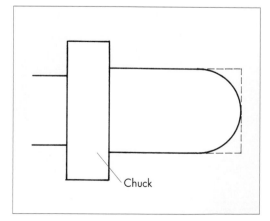

Fig 7.1

Fig 7.2

Figs 7.1 and 7.2 Cut away the corners to produce a sweeping curve from the centre of the end face to the side face.

produced a continuous curve with no flats (*see* Chapter 5 for a discussion of design principles). Make any further adjustments necessary until the desired shape of curve has been obtained. In this example you should aim for a diameter of 1in (25mm) and a dome depth of ⅝in (16mm).

7 When the finishing cuts have been made, sand and finish.

8 Bring the tool rest around to the side of the wood once more so that it is parallel to the axis.

9 Decide where the exact point of parting off should occur. Ideally this should be at the point where the sweep of the curve *just*

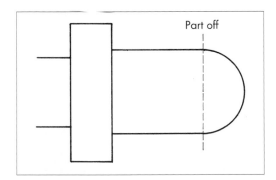

Fig 7.3 Part off at the point where the curve meets the side.

becomes parallel with the side face, so that there is no flat area (*see* Fig 7.3). In this example, it should be ⅝in (16mm) from the tailstock end of the blank (peak of the dome).

10 Part off at the desired depth (*see* Fig 7.4), and sand and finish the back of the brooch by hand.

11 Using a strong adhesive, glue on a suitably sized brooch back. This should be large enough to extend as far across the back of the brooch as possible without being seen from the front (*see* Chapter 16 for further details of jewellery findings).

SIDE-GRAIN BROOCH

In the case of the side-grain brooch (unlike the end-grain), two brooches are turned simultaneously from one blank which has previously been sawn in half lengthwise and reassembled using a paper joint. The advantage of using this method is that for the same amount of time and effort you get two brooches instead of one. A more important advantage, however, is that you are not limited to a spherical shape; the brooch can be any shape you like. In the remainder of

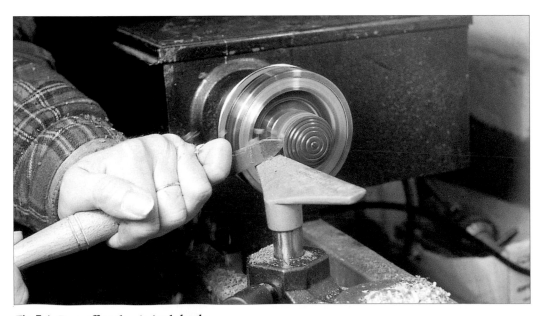

Fig 7.4 Part off at the desired depth.

this chapter we will be looking at two popular shapes for brooches: the apple and the pear. (Using the same technique, all manner of shapes can be produced, e.g. ovals, teardrops, hearts, etc.)

APPLE BROOCH

1 Select a suitable piece of timber, preferably dense, fine grained, and of the chosen colour. Convert this to a blank 2¾in (70mm) long, and 1⅜in (35mm) wide.

2 Using a bandsaw, cut this in half lengthwise and glue back together with a piece of thick paper in between. Leave to dry.

3 Mount this on the lathe between centres and rough down to a cylinder.

4 Turn a spigot at one end of the correct size to fit a contracting collet chuck or similar device for holding wood at one end.

5 Remount the blank in the chuck. Fig 7.5 illustrates how the apple shape will be cut from the blank.

6 Bring the tool rest round so that it is parallel with the end face.

7 Using a bowl gouge, slowly and carefully cut away a dish shape in the end face (*see* Figs 7.6 and 7.7). This is to represent the hollow in the top of the apple.

8 When you are satisfied that you have hollowed out enough from the end face (only a shallow hollow is required), bring the tool rest around to the side again so that it is once more parallel to the axis.

9 Using the bowl gouge, remove the corner from the end face so that a sweeping curve is obtained from the edge of the hollow to the side face (*see* Figs 7.8 and 7.9). This curve represents roughly the top third of the apple.

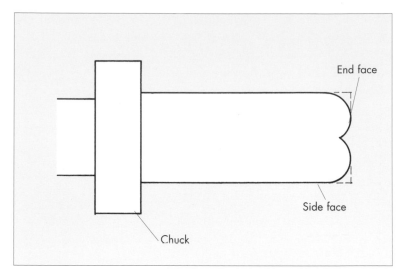

Fig 7.5 The intended shape of the apple to be cut from the blank.

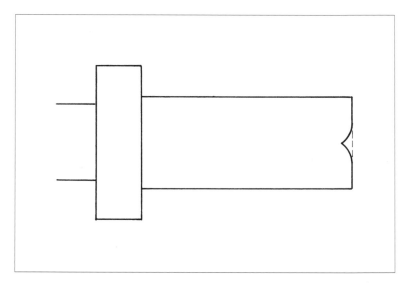

Fig 7.6

Figs 7.6 and 7.7 Cut away a hollow in the end face.   **Fig 7.7**

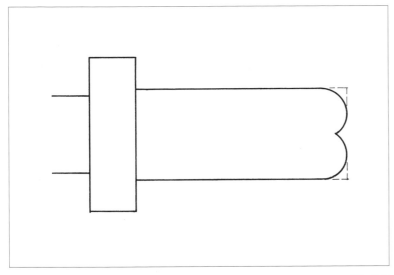

Fig 7.8

Figs 7.8 and 7.9 Remove the corner from the end face so that a sweeping curve is obtained from the hollow to the side face.   **Fig 7.9**

10 Now continue to extend the curve towards the base of the apple, trying to ensure there are no flats (*see* Figs 7.10 and 7.11).

11 Keep checking the shape of your apple as you go. Remember that apples come in all shapes and sizes, so the exact shape is not critical. For a blank of these dimensions, an appropriate length would be 1in (25mm) and the widest part of the apple would be approximately 1⅛in (29mm). Continue to extend the curve around the base of the apple until it remains attached to the blank by a small spigot (*see* Figs 7.12 and 7.13).

12 Sand and finish.

13 Part off, and separate the two halves. If you have used a glue that is too strong, you may find this difficult. A good solution is to insert a thin-bladed knife or a sharpened screwdriver into the joint.

14 Sand and finish the two brooch backs by hand, and fix to each a metal brooch back, as described on page 47.

15 Using a pillar drill, drill a small hole in the hollow of the apple, just behind the flat back, to receive the stalk. The size of the hole is not critical and will, of course,

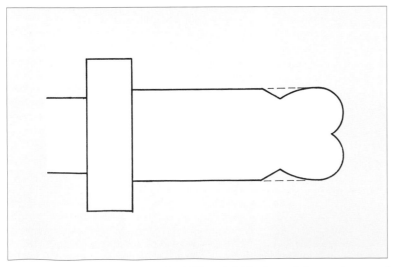

Fig 7.10   **Figs 7.10 and 7.11 Extend the curve towards the base of the apple.**   **Fig 7.11**

NOTE 7.1 When turning the stalks remember that it is not necessary to adhere to accurate biological proportions. Make the stalk considerably larger than it would be on a real piece of fruit. The reason for this is twofold: firstly, a correctly proportioned stalk would be too delicate, prone to break and difficult to turn; secondly, and more importantly, these are stylized fruit – the stalk, being a salient feature, needs to be emphasized.

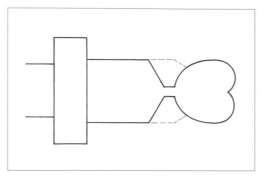

Fig 7.12 **Extend the curve around the base of the apple until it remains attached to the rest of the blank only by a thin spigot.**

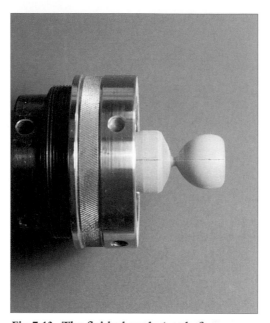

Fig 7.13 **The finished apple (made from amarello) remains attached by a thin spigot.**

depend on the overall apple size. For this example it should be approximately ⅛in (3mm). It is possible to drill the hole by hand if you do not have a pillar drill.

16 Using a small piece of scrap wood of the same type as you have used for the apple, turn a small stalk between centres. Make sure that the bottom end of the stalk is the right size to fit into the hole that you have drilled in the top of the apple, i.e. tapered to just less than ⅛in (3mm). (*See* Note 7.1.)

17 Glue the stalk into the hole and the brooch is complete (*see* Figs 7.14 and 7.15).

PEAR BROOCH

The procedure for this brooch is very similar to that of the apple, the only difference being that because there is no hollow in the top of a pear, it is not absolutely necessary to have a collet chuck (or similar) to hold the wood at one end only. It is possible to turn the entire object between centres. It is obviously easier with a collet chuck because it makes the top end of the pear more accessible and it can therefore be completely finished before parting off. Nevertheless, for those people who are limited to turning between centres, this is a straightforward project and a satisfactory alternative to the apple.

Fig 7.14 **A collection of apple brooches. Clockwise from the left: yew, amarello, Brazilian purple heart, stained sycamore.**

Fig 7.15 **A small 'whole' apple (made from rosewood), mounted on a stick pin.**

1 Follow steps 1 to 3 on page 48.

2 If you intend to turn the pear between centres, proceed to shape the blank carefully, using a bowl gouge. If you intend using a collet chuck (or similar), follow steps 4 and 5 on page 48.

3 The precise size and shape of the pear will depend on personal choice, but a suitable overall length would be 1¼in (32mm), and the widest part, 1⅛in (29mm). Continue to cut until the desired shape is achieved. Check to see that the curves are continuous and that there are no flats. When you are satisfied with the shape, begin to part off at the base but do not part off completely. Leave the pear attached to the blank by a small spigot (*see* Fig 7.16).

4 Sand and finish.

5 Follow steps 13 to 16 on pages 49–50.

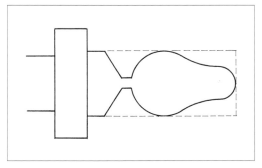

Fig 7.16 The pear brooch is made in a similar fashion to the apple brooch.

Fig 7.17 A pear brooch made from stained oak, with a brass stalk.

Fig 7.18 A purple-heart brooch decorated with beading.

Fig 7.19 A purple-heart brooch inlaid with a quartz stone.

Fig 7.20 An oval, side-grain, ebony brooch with inlaid silver wire.

DECORATIVE TECHNIQUES

There is no need for further decoration with the apple and pear brooches, unless you wish to stain the wood (*see* Chapter 11). However, for other brooches, a variety of techniques may be used to good effect. Beading, for example, can look good. Also, inlaid wire, use of glass beads or gemstones etc. The photos at the end of this chapter illustrate some of these techniques (*see* Chapter 14 for further details on decorative techniques).

8

Bangles

▌ Hoop bangle   ▌ Decorative techniques
▌ Broad bangle

ESSENTIAL EQUIPMENT	RECOMMENDED EQUIPMENT
▌ Lathe ▌ Basic turning tools ▌ Screw chuck ▌ Callipers	▌ Pillar drill ▌ Expanding dovetail collet chuck

LEVEL OF SKILL: Novice

THIS CHAPTER describes how to make two basic designs of bangle. The first may be described as a 'hoop' style, where the cross section is circular or oval (*see* Figs 8.1 and 8.2). The second is a broader design where the cross section has a flat base (*see* Figs 8.3 and 8.4).

HOOP BANGLE

1 Select a suitable piece of timber. Since bangles are relatively large (compared to earrings and brooches, for example), there is not the same necessity for the chosen timber to be dense and fine grained. Many timbers, such as oak and acacia, for example, have well-defined growth rings which can be very attractive, especially when stained (*see* Chapter 11). This makes them particularly suitable for bangles.

The dimensions of the desired bangle will obviously vary according to the wrist size of the wearer, and personal taste. These instructions describe the creation of a bangle of the following dimensions:

External diameter: 3½in (89mm)
Internal diameter: 2½in (64mm)
Width of hoop: ½in (13mm)

Prepare a circular blank of 4in (102mm) diameter and ¾in (20mm) depth.

2 Drill a hole all the way through the centre of the blank. It is absolutely essential to ensure that this hole is drilled vertically (i.e. at right angles to the face of the blank). If the hole is not drilled vertically, this will cause problems when reverse-chucking, because the blank will not run true. A pillar drill or drill stand is helpful at this point but not crucial.

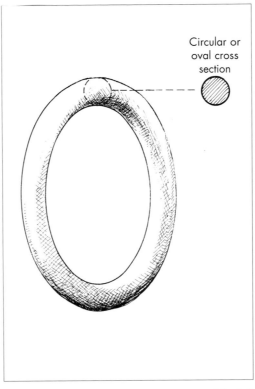

Circular or oval cross section

Fig 8.1

Figs 8.1 and 8.2 The hoop bangle.

Fig 8.2

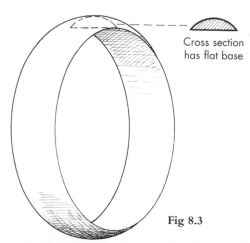

Cross section
has flat base

Fig 8.3

3 Mount the blank on a screw chuck and, with the tool rest parallel to the bed bars, rough down to a cylinder 3½in (89mm).

4 With a skew chisel, true up the end face (*see* Fig 8.5).

5 Move the tool rest so that it is parallel with, and close to, the end face.

Figs 8.3 and 8.4 The broad bangle.

Fig 8.4

Fig 8.5 True up the end face with a skew chisel.

6 Using a pair of dividers, compasses or callipers, mark on the end face a circle to represent the inner diameter of the bangle (*see* Fig 8.6), which in this example is 2½in (64mm).

7 With a parting tool, make a straight cut into the wood with the left-hand edge of the blade on the line that you have just marked. Cut halfway into the depth of the blank. For a bangle of ½in (13mm) thickness, the depth of this cut should be ¼in (6mm). (*See* Figs 8.7 and 8.8.) Then carefully measure the depth to which you have cut. The outer and inner dimensions of the bangle have now been defined and the shaping can begin.

Fig 8.6 Mark a circle on the end face representing the inner diameter of the bangle.

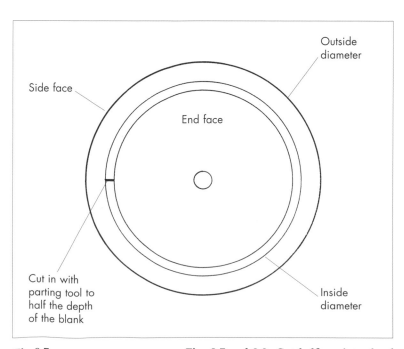

Outside
diameter

Side face

End face

Cut in with
parting tool to
half the depth
of the blank

Inside
diameter

Fig 8.7

Figs 8.7 and 8.8 Cut halfway into the depth of the blank.

Fig 8.8

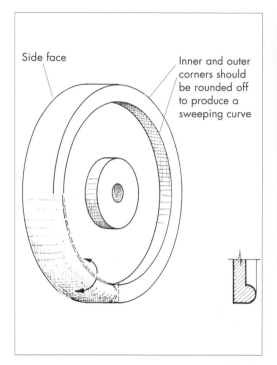

Side face

Inner and outer corners should be rounded off to produce a sweeping curve

Fig 8.9

Fig 8.10

Figs 8.9, 8.10 and 8.11 Remove the inner and outer corners with a bowl gouge.   **Fig 8.11**

8 Keeping the tool rest in the same position, remove the inner and outer corners with a bowl gouge until a sweeping curve is obtained (*see* Figs 8.9, 8.10 and 8.11). The inside and outside curves should be roughly the same, and the end face cross section should now be hemispherical (*see* Fig 8.12). Cut away sufficient wood from the middle of the end face to enable you to sand the inside comfortably without getting fingers caught.

9 Sand and finish this half of the bangle.

10 Remove the blank from the screw chuck and remount the other way round.

11 Repeat steps 6 and 7 but be very careful when cutting into the blank with the parting tool. It is essential that you cut almost halfway through, but not quite through to the cut on the other side. That is why it was necessary to measure the precise depth of the first cut, which in this case was ¼in (6mm).

12 Repeat steps 8 and 9.

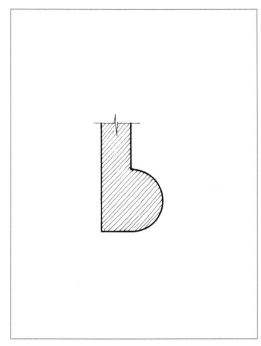

Fig 8.12 The hemispherical cross section through the end face.

13 The bangle is now almost finished and is ready to be parted off. Do this with a parting tool, cutting straight into the wood as before, until you cut right through. (*See* Note 8.1.)

On the inside of the bangle will be a small ridge or jagged edge, the size of which will depend upon how accurately you measured and cut the internal diameter from either side. This ridge can be removed as follows:

14 Turn between centres a cylinder of scrap wood upon which various grades of abrasive paper have been stuck. The diameter of this wood is not important – 1³⁄₁₆–1⁹⁄₁₆in (30–40mm) diameter is quite sufficient (*see* Figs 8.13 and 8.14).

15 With the sanding cylinder mounted between centres, place the bangle so that it encircles it, switch on the lathe, and rotate the inside of the bangle around each grade of abrasive in turn, from the coarsest to the finest. In this way, the rough edge inside the bangle will be removed.

16 Apply the desired finish to the inside of the bangle by hand (*see* Chapter 15).

NOTE 8.1 When you break through to the other side, the bangle will spin away from the remainder of the blank and can sometimes hit the tool rest with some force. In order to prevent the bangle from becoming damaged it is a good idea to tie a piece of cloth securely around the tool rest to cushion any blow. It is important, however, to ensure that there are no loose ends of cloth that could become entangled.

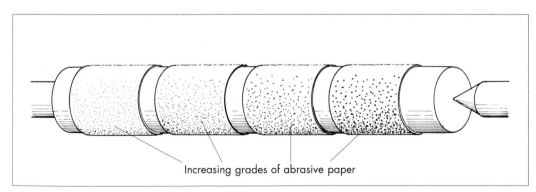

Increasing grades of abrasive paper

Fig 8.13

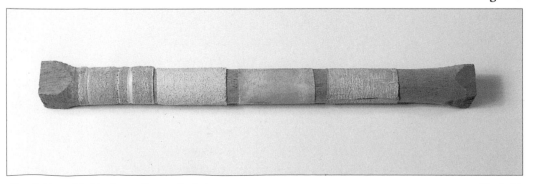

Figs 8.13 and 8.14 A sanding cylinder.

Fig 8.14

BROAD BANGLE

Because the cross section of a broad bangle is not circular, there is scope for a variety of different shapes within the basic design. Fig 8.15 shows some possibilities. Any of these can be made by the following method:

1 The dimensions of the desired bangle may vary, but these instructions describe the creation of a bangle of the following dimensions:

> External diameter: 3½in (89mm)
> Internal diameter: 2⅝in (67mm)
> Width: 1¼in (32mm)

For a bangle of the above dimensions, prepare a circular blank with a diameter of 3¾in (95mm) and a depth of 1½in (38mm).

2 Drill a hole in the centre, but not right the way through.

3 Mount onto a screw chuck.

4 Follow steps 4–7 of the method described for the hoop bangle (above).

5 Before beginning the shaping of the outside, some attention must be given to the cut that has just been made, which defines

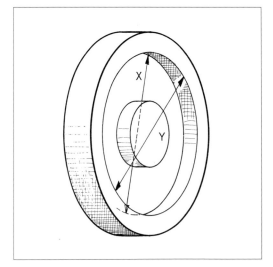

Fig 8.17 Y is the diameter at the point of entry; X is the diameter at the centre; X and Y should be equal.

the inner diameter. Using a pair of internal callipers, measure the diameter of the cut at the point of entry (*see* Fig 8.16). Then measure the diameter at the end of the cut (halfway through the depth of the blank). These two measurements should be exactly the same, i.e. 2⅝in (67mm). If they differ, it means that you have not cut through straight, at right angles to the end face. It is very easy to cut in at a slight angle, without realizing that you have done so. Most often, you will find that your diameter gets narrower as the cut progresses through the wood. At this stage it is important to true up this inner cut so that it runs parallel to the side face, and this will be achieved when both diameter measurements are the same, i.e. 2⅝in (67mm). (*See* Fig 8.17.)

6 With a skew chisel, make a fine finishing cut along the inside diameter.

7 Now the shaping of the outside can begin. Keeping the tool rest in the same position, and using a bowl gouge, start to remove the outer corner bit by bit, working outwards all the time. You should aim to achieve a sweeping curve which begins from ⅟₁₆in (2mm) outside the inner diameter and ends at the centre line of the side face (*see* Figs 8.18 and 8.19). Try to ensure that the sweep of the curve is continuous with no flat areas. The end of the curve at the centre of the side face should be the highest point of the curve.

8 Sand and finish the inside and outside cuts. At this stage the bangle is half complete.

9 Remove the blank from the screw chuck and reverse onto an expanding dovetail collet. A 2½in (64mm) collet will expand nicely into the inner diameter of the bangle that you have cut. (*See* Note 8.2.)

10 Make sure that the blank is running true, then repeat steps 4 and 5 (above). (*See* Note 8.3.)

NOTE 8.2 To protect the finished inner edge of the bangle from the hard edges of the collet jaws, wrap a thin strip of cardboard or a wide elastic band around the jaws of the collet before positioning the bangle on the chuck.

NOTE 8.3 Unlike the method for the hoop bangle, when cutting the inner diameter you need to cut right through to the other side (*see* Fig 8.20). This is made possible by the fact that the bangle is held securely by the dovetail collet and will not be released as soon as you cut through. Tidy up the inner diameter line. If you have not been completely accurate with your cuts, it is likely that there will be a slight ridge on the inside. This can easily be removed at this stage with a parting tool or skew chisel.

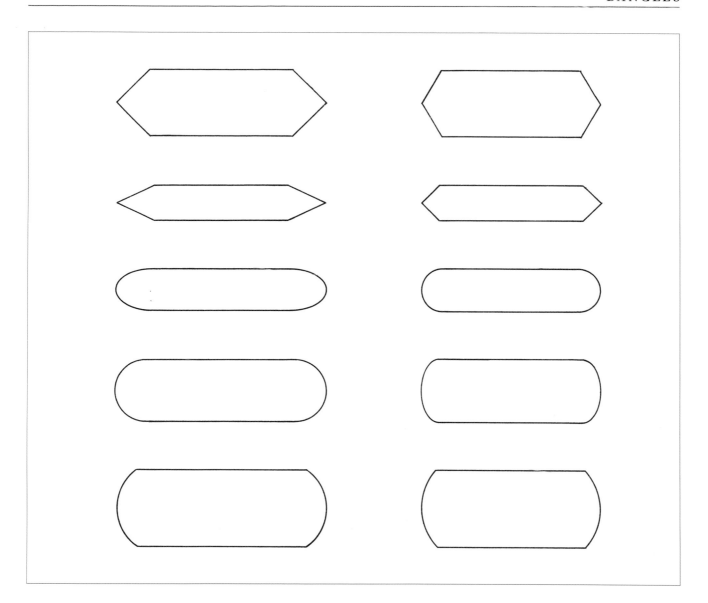

Fig 8.15 A variety
of possible broad
bangle shapes.
Bangles can vary
both in their depth
and in the shape of
their outer edge.

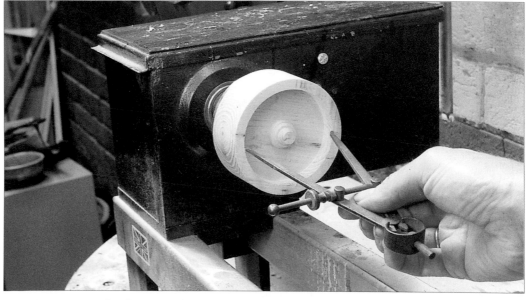

Fig 8.16 Measure the diameter of the cut at the point of entry.

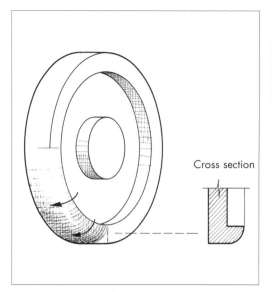

Cross section

Fig 8.18   **Figs 8.18 and 8.19 Gradually cut away the outer corner, working outwards all the time, to produce a sweeping curve.**   **Fig 8.19**

Fig 8.20 Cut right through to the other side.

11 Now shape the second half of the outside face as before (step 7 above).

12 Sand and finish the second halves of the inside and outside edges. The bangle is now complete and can be removed from the chuck.

See Note 8.4.

DECORATIVE TECHNIQUES

Before beginning your bangle you may wish to consider using some form of decoration. Examples may include beading, scorch rings, inlaying with wire or wood bands etc. Refer to Chapters 12, 13 and 14 for more ideas.

NOTE 8.4 If you do not possess an expanding dovetail collet, the same technique can be used following the method described for the hoop bangle, where the blank is reversed onto the screw chuck. You will have to drill your centre hole straight through the circular blank as in step 2 for the hoop bangle (*see* page 53). The disadvantage of reverse chucking onto a screw chuck is that unless your initial hole has been drilled extremely accurately, the blank will not run absolutely true when reversed. This can be rectified, but a more difficult problem to overcome is that, unless you are absolutely precise in cutting your inner diameter from both sides, it is likely that there will be a ridge on the inside face where your two cuts did not quite meet up. This ridge can be difficult to remove because the bangle is no longer supported on the screw chuck as soon as you cut right through. The only way the inside surface can be tidied up is by using a sanding cylinder (*see* page 57). This will work, but it is much more time consuming to use a sanding cylinder on a broad bangle with a flat inside face than it is for a hoop bangle, because the area to be sanded is much greater. If you intend to make a lot of broad bangles, it would certainly be worth investing in an expanding dovetail collet since it makes the whole process more accurate, and therefore easier and quicker.

C H A P T E R

9

Rings

■ Hoop ring   ■ Decorative techniques
■ Broad ring   ■ Alternative materials

ESSENTIAL EQUIPMENT	RECOMMENDED EQUIPMENT
■ Lathe ■ Basic turning tools ■ Callipers ■ Contracting collet chuck (or similar device)	■ Morse taper drill chuck ■ ⅝in (16mm) drill bit

LEVEL OF SKILL: Novice

N THIS CHAPTER I shall be describing the methods for two basic designs of ring. The first is a 'hoop' ring, where the cross section is circular (*see* Figs 9.1 and 9.2), and the second is a broad ring where the cross section has a flat base (*see* Figs 9.3 and 9.4). Hoop rings are fine when only a narrow band is required. However, in cases of wider bands, this design is unsuitable because, with a ring of circular cross section where width equals depth, the increased depth required would cause the ring to protrude too far around the finger. This would be impractical and uncomfortable. With the design for the broad ring described in this chapter, the flat base of the cross section effectively removes some of the depth while retaining the width. Both the methods described are fairly simple, and enable several rings to be produced from one blank in a relatively short space of time.

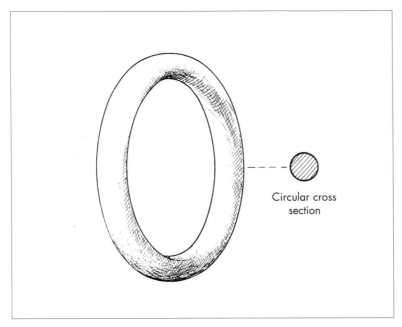

Circular cross section

Fig 9.1

Figs 9.1 and 9.2 A hoop ring.

Fig 9.2

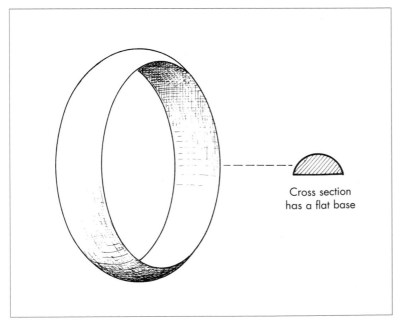

Cross section has a flat base

Fig 9.3

Figs 9.3 and 9.4 A broad ring.

Fig 9.4

HOOP RING

1 Select a suitable piece of timber with the grain running parallel to its length. (Since rings are very small items, be sure to select timber that is very dense and fine grained, e.g. ebony.) The desired dimensions of the ring will vary according to the wearer's finger size and personal taste. The following instructions describe the creation of a ring of the following dimensions:

External diameter: 1$\frac{5}{16}$in (24mm)
Internal diameter: $\frac{11}{16}$in (17mm)
Width: $\frac{1}{8}$in (3mm)

For a ring of the above dimensions, the blank should have a cross section of 1$\frac{1}{8}$in (29mm). The length is not critical and will depend upon the number of rings you wish to make. This method is suitable for turning several rings from one blank. A length of 2$\frac{3}{8}$in (60mm) would be suitable for this.

2 Mount the blank on the lathe between centres and rough down to a cylinder.

3 Turn a spigot at one end with a diameter to fit a contracting collet chuck, or similar. (Alternatively, the wooden faceplate method of chucking, as described in Chapter 4, could be employed.)

4 Mount the blank in the contracting collet chuck and finish turning the cylinder to the required diameter, which in this example is 1$\frac{5}{16}$in (24mm).

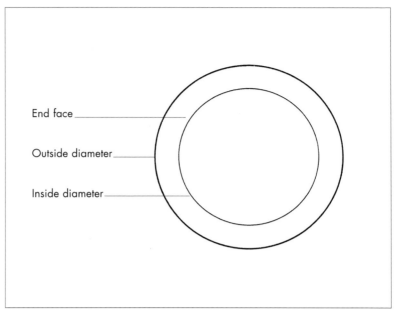

Fig 9.5 Mark the inside diameter of the ring on the end face of the blank.

5 Bring the tool rest around so that it is parallel with the end face of the blank. With the lathe turning, mark on the end face the inside diameter of the ring, which is determined by the width of the future wearer's finger. This can be done with a pair of dividers, callipers, or something similar (*see* Fig 9.5).

6 Using a parting tool, cut into the end face *gently* in order to remove some of the wood from inside the inner marked circle (*see* Fig 9.6). Cut to a depth that will equal the width of the ring, or slightly deeper. In this example, cut to at least $\frac{1}{8}$in (3mm). (*See* Note 9.1.)

NOTE 9.1 Take care when making this cut. Cutting into end grain in this fashion can cause digs which may cause the blank to become slightly unseated in the chuck. To avoid this, ensure that your tool is sharp, and do not attempt to remove too much wood at once. Check that the sides of the hole are parallel along its length. Failure to do so will result in one side of the ring having a different internal diameter to the other side. Alternatively, it is possible to bore a hole in the end face, using a drill bit of the appropriate size mounted in a drill chuck that is fitted into the tailstock (*see* the method for the broad ring on pages 67–68).

Fig 9.6 Cut into the end face gently.

7 Using a bowl gouge, remove the inner and outer corners of the ring to produce a circular sweep from the outside diameter through to the inside (*see* Figs 9.7, 9.8 and 9.9). As you cut, remember that you are aiming eventually for a circular cross section, so the end face, at this stage, should be hemispherical (*see* Fig 9.10).

8 Sand and apply a finish to this side of the ring.

9 Move the tool rest back to the side face of the blank and mark out the desired width of the ring (which will be roughly equal to the depth). In this example it will be ⅛in (3mm).

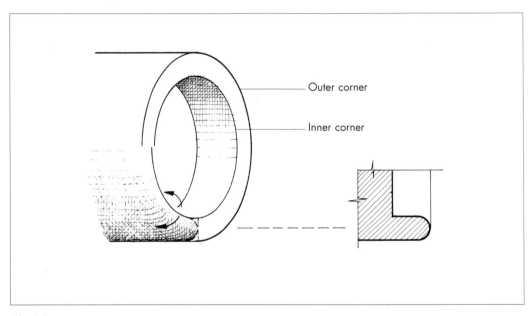

Outer corner

Inner corner

Fig 9.7

Figs 9.7, 9.8 and 9.9 Remove the inner and outer corners.

Fig 9.8

Fig 9.9

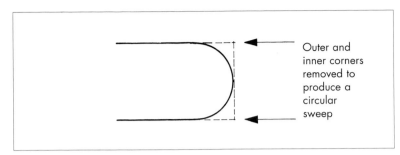

Fig 9.10 A cross section of the end face.

10 Remove some wood to the left of this to give you some room for manoeuvre (*see* Figs 9.11 and 9.12).

11 Now shape the left-hand outer corner (*see* Fig 9.13). Sand and finish.

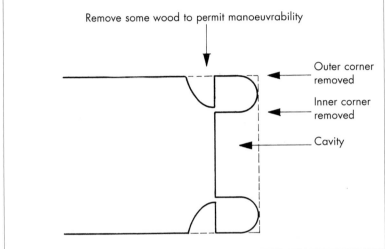

Fig 9.11 A cross section of the blank.

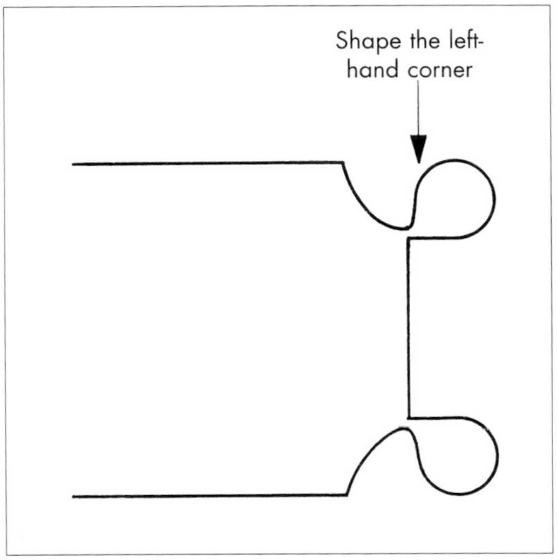

Fig 9.13 A cross section of the blank.

Fig 9.12 Remove some wood to give yourself some room for manoeuvre.

12 At this stage there is only a small piece of wood holding the ring to the rest of the blank. This is removed as the lower corner is shaped (*see* Fig 9.14). This cut is best done with a skew chisel.

13 When you finally cut through the lower corner, the ring will become detached from the blank. There will be a rough edge at the point where you have cut through. There are a number of different methods that can be used for tidying up this edge. Possibly the simplest is to turn a tapered spigot from a piece of scrap wood. The diamcter of the end of the tapered spigot is critical and should be the same as the internal diameter of the ring. In this example the spigot should taper to just under $^{11}/_{16}$in (17mm). Insert the ring over the end of the spigot so that the rough edge is facing outwards (*see* Fig 9.15). Ensure that the edge of the ring projects slightly beyond the end of the spigot in order to enable easy access. (Double-sided Sellotape wrapped around the end of the spigot helps to secure the ring firmly.) Sand and finish.

Alternatively, a sanding cylinder can be used, as follows: Between centres, turn a thin cylinder that has a smaller diameter than the ring. Using a suitable adhesive, stick strips of abrasive paper in increasing grades along its length to produce a sanding cylinder (*see* Figs

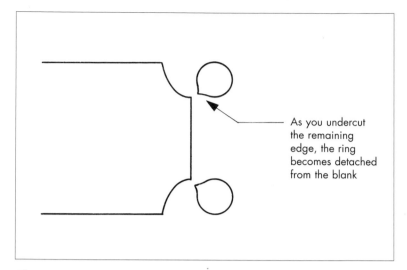

Fig 9.14 A cross section of the blank.

As you undercut the remaining edge, the ring becomes detached from the blank

8.13 and 8.14 on page 57, where this method is also described). When the glue has set, place the ring over the cylinder and, with the cylinder firmly mounted between centres and the lathe running, grip the ring and move it gently over the abrasive paper, gradually moving to the finest grade. Make sure that you sand only the rough edge, since the other sides have already been finished. When the ring has been sanded to your satisfaction, remove it from the sanding cylinder and apply a finish to the appropriate areas by hand (*see* Chapter 15).

Further rings can now be turned in the same way from the same blank. *See* Note 9.2.

NOTE 9.2 For those people who possess ring-forming tools, a hoop ring can be made in the same way as 'captive' rings. For some, this may be an easier and quicker method.

Fig 9.15 The ring is mounted onto a tapered spigot to finish off the rough edge.

BROAD RING

The method for making broad rings is similar to that for making hoop rings, but is probably slightly easier.

1 Follow steps 1 to 5 from the hoop-ring method outlined above.

2 With the tool rest parallel to the end face of the blank, remove wood from inside the marked circle (the inner diameter of the ring) (*see* Fig 9.16). This can be done using a parting tool, as described in the hoop-ring method. An easier technique is to bore a hole using a drill bit mounted in a morse taper drill chuck that has been inserted into the tailstock (*see* Fig 9.17). Unless you are very lucky, it is unlikely that you will have a drill bit of exactly the right size, so to begin with you will probably have to use one slightly smaller than the required internal diameter, which in this case is $^{11}\!/_{16}$in (17mm). Then remove the rest of the wood with a parting tool. At least the drill will have done most of the work for you and you will be certain of having a hole with exactly parallel sides. Another advantage of using a drill to bore the hole is that, apart from being easier than working away with a parting tool, you can drill in quite deep and produce a hole for a number of rings on the same blank, thus saving considerable time. A $^5\!/_8$in (16mm) drill bit is about the right size for a small diameter ring. For a ring of average internal diameter, a $^5\!/_8$in (16mm) bit will probably be the nearest size and the remaining wood can then be removed with a parting tool. The depth to which you drill will depend upon the desired width of the ring and the number of rings you intend to make from this blank. (*See* Note 9.3.)

3 Remove wood from the outer corner only. Cut in a sweeping curve, working from the outside inwards (*see* Fig 9.18).

4 Sand and finish the inside and the outside.

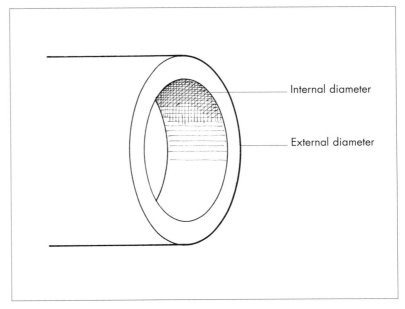

Fig 9.16 **Remove the wood from inside the marked circle.**

Internal diameter

External diameter

Fig 9.17 **Bore a hole using a drill bit.**

NOTE 9.3 When boring holes in this fashion always make sure that the lathe is running at the lowest possible speed. Proceed very slowly. Failure to do so may result in the wood over-heating. This in turn can sometimes cause it to split.

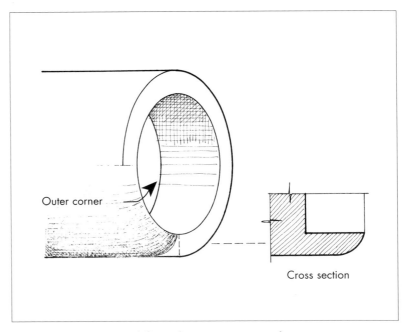

Outer corner

Cross section

Fig 9.18 **Remove wood from the outer corner only.**

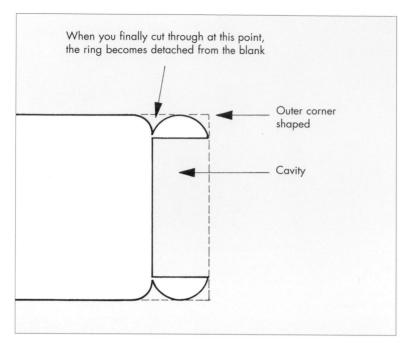

When you finally cut through at this point, the ring becomes detached from the blank

Outer corner shaped

Cavity

Fig 9.19

Fig 9.20

Figs 9.19 and 9.20 Shape the other outside edge to match the first.

5 Now shape the other outside edge of the ring to match the first side (*see* Figs 9.19 and 9.20). When you finally cut through to the inner hole the ring will be released from the rest of the blank. Once again there will be a rough edge which can be tidied up using the procedure described in the hoop-ring method.

The end result should be a broad ring with a flat base in the cross section.

As before, a number of further rings can be cut from the same blank.

DECORATIVE TECHNIQUES

Some of the techniques suggested below can be used effectively to improve the general appearance of a ring. However, many can only be used with rings over a certain minimum width.

BEADING

Cutting one or two beads on the surface of the ring can enhance the overall appearance, and can give a more interesting texture. Dense, fine-grained woods are most suitable.

WIRE INLAY

One of the most effective ways of decorating a ring is to inlay a circle of wire around its circumference (*see* Fig 9.21, and *see* Chapter 12 for details). A wide ring could accommodate two circles of inlaid wire.

Fig 9.21 An ebony ring decorated with a wire inlay.

Fig 9.22 An ebony ring decorated with an inlaid haematite bead.

INLAYING GLASS BEADS

Small glass or mineral beads can be effectively used to decorate rings (*see* Fig 9.22, and *see* Chapter 14 for details).

STAINING

Pale woods can be attractively stained to any desired colour (*see* Chapter 11).

Suggestions for further decorative techniques can be found in Chapter 14.

ALTERNATIVE MATERIALS

Apart from wood, there are various other materials that can be turned to form rings. Tagua nut is one example, horn is another (*see* Chapter 17 for details).

CHAPTER

10
Necklaces

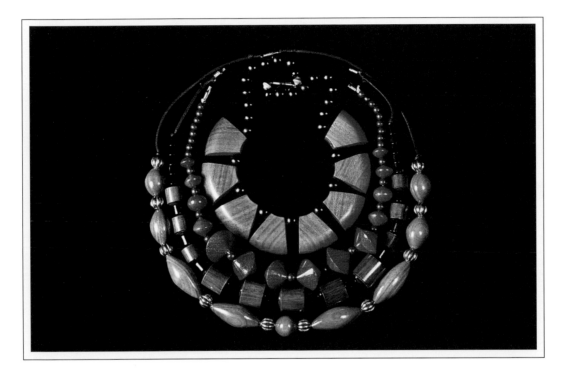

■ Beads   ■ Threading up
■ Turning beads

ESSENTIAL EQUIPMENT	RECOMMENDED EQUIPMENT
■ Lathe ■ Basic turning tools ■ Screw chuck ■ Wooden faceplate *or* contracting collet chuck (or similar device) ■ Callipers ■ Small drill bit	■ Morse taper drill chuck *or* pillar drill

LEVEL OF SKILL: Novice

IKE OTHER TYPES of jewellery, necklaces can take many forms. The simplest, perhaps, is the pendant. This usually consists of some decorative object suspended by a chain or cord of some description that is worn around the neck. In this chapter, however, I have chosen to describe necklaces that are made from strings of turned wooden beads. (*See* Note 10.1.)

BEADS

There is no limit to the variety of shapes and forms that beads can take (*see* Fig 10.1). The only constraints are pragmatic ones; for example, the beads must not be too heavy or cumbersome if they are to be worn comfortably. Apart from that, the only limit is your own imagination.

Before embarking upon the making of a necklace, the following considerations might be made:

WHAT SIZE SHOULD THE BEADS BE?

This is a matter of personal preference. Making very small beads can be a good way of using up tiny offcuts of wood that would probably be too small for anything else. Remember, though, that if the beads are very small, you will need a great many of them for a necklace, which will be time consuming. If time is not a problem then you can make them as small as you like. The best way of chucking the tiny scraps of wood suitable for small beads is by gluing the blank to a wooden faceplate (*see* Chapter 4 for details).

NOTE 10.1 In this chapter, the word 'bead' is used in its conventional sense, i.e. a small object – not necessarily round or symmetrical – with a hole passing through it, which is threaded onto a cord of some kind. The word should not be confused with the term 'beading' commonly used by woodturners, which refers to the cutting of a semicircular ring into the outer surface of an object.

Fig 10.1 A selection of beads of different designs.

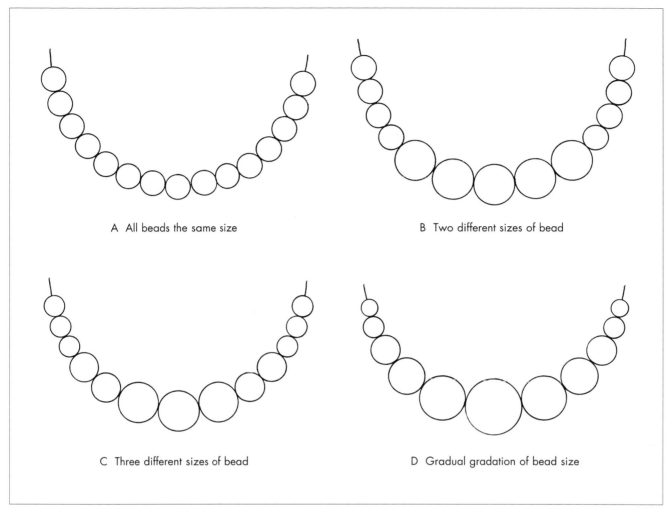

Fig 10.2 Various ways of combining different bead sizes in necklaces.

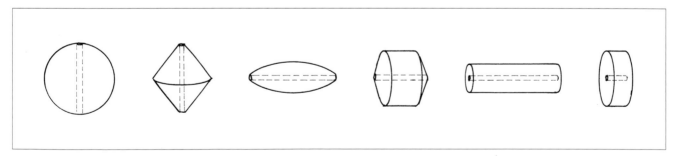

Fig 10.3 Various bead shapes.

Large beads can be very eye-catching, but be careful not to make them *too* large or they will be too heavy to be worn comfortably.

SHOULD ALL THE BEADS BE THE SAME SIZE?

Again, this is a matter of personal preference. Quite an attractive effect can be obtained by varying the size of the beads, and stringing them so that the largest ones hang in the middle. Fig 10.2 shows some possibilities.

WHAT SHAPE SHOULD THE BEADS BE?

Beads do not have to be round. They can be any shape (*see* Fig 10.3).

SHOULD ALL THE BEADS BE THE SAME SHAPE?

Different-shaped beads can be mixed successfully within one necklace. For example, oval beads of different widths and lengths can look attractive. However, too many different shapes within one necklace can sometimes look messy.

HOW MANY BEADS WILL I NEED?

This will depend upon the size of the beads and the overall desired length of the necklace. The desired length of the necklace is divided by the intended width of each bead to give a rough indication of how many beads will be required. Of course this calculation becomes more complicated if you intend to use beads of different sizes and/or spacers (*see* below). Remember that it is not always necessary to have beads filling the entire length of the cord. Some of the illustrations later in this chapter show examples of necklaces where only part of the cord contains beads.

WHAT SORT OF WOOD SHOULD BE USED?

The normal considerations apply here. The most suitable woods are those with a fine grain, a good colour, and which take a good polish (*see* Chapter 3 for further details).

Remember also that some materials other than wood are ideal for beads. Cow horn is a good example (*see* Chapter 17 for details on turning alternative materials).

CAN I MIX TWO OR MORE WOODS IN ONE NECKLACE?

Combining two or more woods of different colours can be done very successfully, especially when coordinating colours to match an outfit, for example.

WILL I NEED 'SPACERS' BETWEEN THE BEADS?

Spacers are smaller beads that are inserted between larger ones in order to provide balance and to enable the larger beads to hang correctly. Spacers are not always necessary. It will depend on the shape of your larger beads and the effect you are trying to achieve. You can, of course, turn your own spacers but this is very time consuming. I usually use small glass, wood, or metal beads inserted between the larger, turned beads.

When you have considered the above questions, you are ready to start. On pages 79–80 there are photographs showing necklaces made from a variety of different beads in different designs and combinations. These may provide inspiration.

TURNING BEADS

There are two different types of bead that I have chosen to describe, and each is made in a different way. The first type is turned from a long cylinder of wood with the grain running parallel to the axis (i.e. spindle turning). Although the shape may vary from one design to the next, these beads all have one thing in common: they all have a circular cross section.

The second type of bead is made very differently. A flat cylinder of wood is attached to a screw chuck or faceplate with the grain running at right angles to the lathe bed (i.e. normal faceplate turning). After shaping, a ring is then formed, removed from the lathe and cut into small, equal segments. Each segment is a bead. Such beads do not have a circular cross section, and are flat on the back. The holes are drilled at the top through the sides so that each bead is suspended below the thread.

The two types of bead are now described in turn.

BEADS WITH A CIRCULAR CROSS SECTION

1 Having selected the chosen wood (preferably dense and fine grained) and decided upon the size (diameter) of the beads to be made, convert the wood into a square cross section of the appropriate size, using a

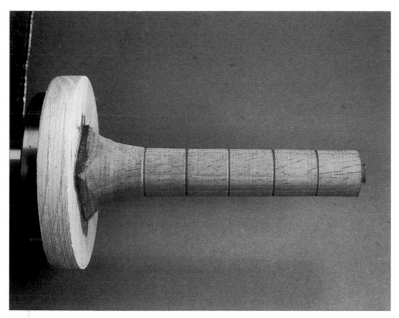

Fig 10.4 Make a series of grooves along the cylinder, each one representing the length of a bead.

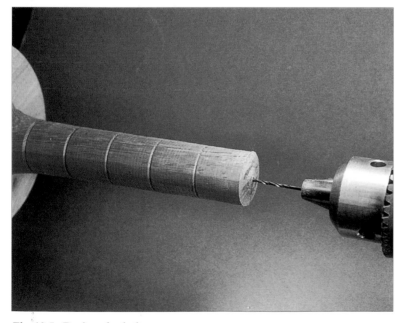

Fig 10.5 Boring the hole.

NOTE 10.2 If you do not possess a morse taper drill bit, the holes can be drilled afterwards using a pillar drill or even a hand drill, but it is much easier and quicker to do it using the method described above.

bandsaw. In other words, if your beads are to be ¾in (20mm) in diameter, your blank should be just slightly larger than ¾in (20mm) square. As stated earlier, beads can be any size and shape, but these instructions describe the creation of an oval bead that is 1in (25mm) long and ⅝in (16mm) wide. The length of the blank is not critical. Ideally it should be long enough to enable you to turn several beads from the one piece, but not so

long that it cannot be turned easily while supported at one end only. For a blank of 1⅛in (29mm) cross section, a length of approximately 4¾in (121mm) would be fine.

2 Decide upon the method of chucking. I would recommend one of the following: *either* glue the blank to the centre of a wooden faceplate or, using a four-prong drive centre, rough the blank down to a cylinder, turn a spigot at one end, then reverse this onto a contracting collet chuck (for details of chucking options, *see* Chapter 4). The method of chucking is not important, so long as the wood is adequately supported.

3 Bring up the tailstock for additional support and true up the cylinder if necessary.

4 Having decided upon the desired *length* of each bead – in this example 1in (25mm) – mark this distance off in series along the cylinder by cutting small grooves with a parting tool (*see* Fig 10.4).

5 Mark the centre line of each segment with a pencil.

6 Remove the revolving tailstock and insert a morse taper drill bit into the tailstock support. Using a small drill bit, and with the lathe running at its slowest speed, bore a hole through the end segment by slowly winding the tailstock closer to the headstock (*see* Fig 10.5). The drilled hole should be *at least* as long as the intended bead – in this example, 1in (25mm). However, you can drill deep enough for two or more beads at once if you wish to save time. The size of the drill bit will depend on the size of the cord you intend to use which, in turn, is determined by the bead size. (*See* Note 10.2.)

7 Replace the revolving tailstock. You may need it to provide additional support, depending on the overall length and width of the blank and the method of chucking.

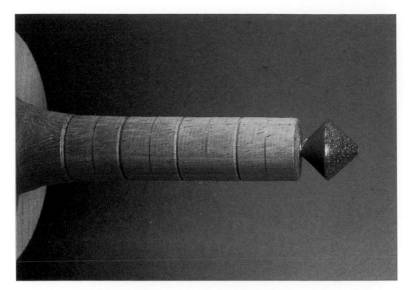

Fig 10.6 A completed bead on the end of the blank.

Fig 10.7 Some examples of beads with a circular cross section.

Fig 10.8 True up the end face using a skew chisel.

8 Now proceed to shape the bead at the extreme right-hand end of the blank (*see* Fig 10.6). This is best done with a skew chisel.

9 When the bead is almost completely shaped but is still attached to the rest of the blank by a thin spigot, sand and apply the desired finish (*see* Chapter 15).

10 Part off carefully.

11 Repeat the above for all the remaining segments on the blank.

It is likely that you will not have obtained enough beads from this blank alone. This being the case, the above procedure should be repeated until enough beads have been turned. If you have decided to use beads of varying sizes, allow for this when roughing down the next blank, making the diameter slightly larger or smaller than the previous one. Remember, in this case, to adjust the width of your marked segments accordingly, if you wish the rest of the beads to be the same shape.

BEADS TURNED FROM A RING

The size and shape of the beads may vary, and the size of the blank will vary accordingly. In the example described below, beads of the following dimensions are produced:

   Length: 1in (25mm)
   Minimum width: ⁷⁄₁₆in (11mm)
   Maximum width: 1³⁄₁₆in (30mm)
   Depth: ³⁄₈in (10mm)

1 Having chosen the desired wood, convert it into a circular blank with the grain running across (as for normal faceplate turning). The depth of the blank should be ½in (25mm). This depth is not critical, but if it was much thicker than this there would be a lot of wastage, and if it was much thinner it would be too small to be attached securely to a screw chuck.

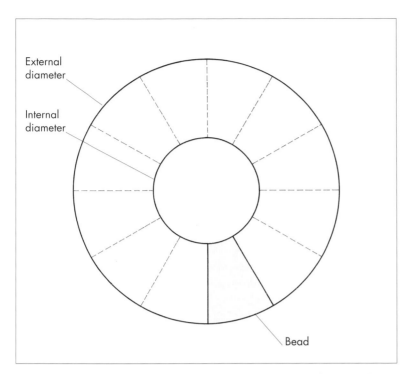

Fig 10.9 The turned ring is sawn into equal segments to form beads.

The diameter is not critical either, and it depends on the desired length of the beads. In this example it will be 3in (76mm).

2 Drill a hole through the centre and attach the blank to a screw chuck.

3 Rough down the edges to a cylinder.

Fig 10.10 Cut a groove representing the internal diameter of the outer ring.

4 True up the end face using a skew chisel (*see* Fig 10.8).

5 Bring the tool rest around so that it is parallel with the end face. Mark a circle on the end face of 1in (25mm) diameter. This will become the internal diameter of the ring. The exact diameter of this circle will depend on the overall dimensions of the blank and is partly determined by the desired length of each bead. This is best understood by looking at Fig 10.9. If the internal diameter is too small in relation to the external diameter, the beads will be too long.

6 Using a parting tool positioned on the inside of the marked internal diameter, cut a groove. The depth of the groove should be approximately half the depth of the blank after truing up. In this case, with a trued-up blank of ⅜in (10mm) depth, cut a groove ³⁄₁₆in (5mm) deep (*see* Fig 10.10). It is important that you measure (with calipers) the exact diameter for this groove and the depth to which you have cut.

7 Sand and finish this end face, including inside the groove.

8 Remove the blank from the screw chuck, reverse it and remount it so that the finished face is flat against the face of the screw chuck.

9 Using a skew chisel, true up the end face.

10 Using a pencil and callipers, mark on the end face the position of the inner diameter of the ring, i.e. the position of the groove on the other side.

11 Using a skew chisel or bowl gouge, make the end face slightly concave so that the disc of wood becomes narrower towards the marked circle. How much wood you remove from the centre will depend upon the depth of the groove that you cut on the

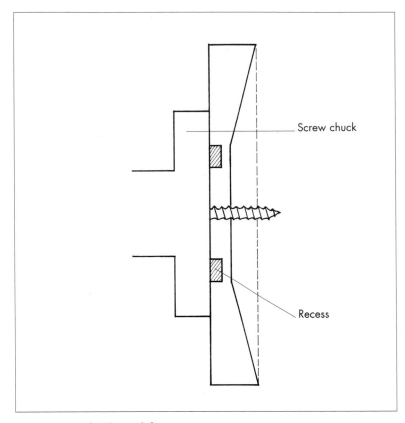

Fig 10.11 Make the end face concave.

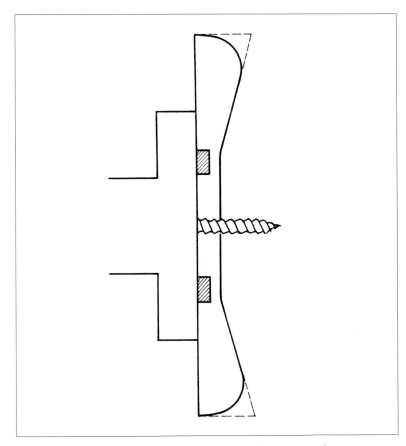

Fig 10.13 Round off the outer corner to produce a smooth curve.

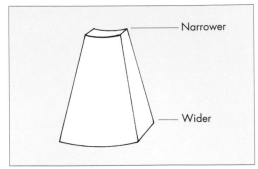

Fig 10.12 The bead is narrower at the top than at the bottom.

other side. In this example, remove wood to a depth of less than ³⁄₁₆in (5mm). You must make sure that you do not cut so deeply that you meet the groove (*see* Fig 10.11)! The reason for the concave shape is to create a bead that is thinner (in depth) at the top than at the bottom. This is not absolutely essential, but it does look better and prevents the beads from looking too clumsy. It also helps them to lie at a pleasing angle (*see* Fig 10.12). In this example, the depth at the top of the bead is ¼in (6mm) and at the bottom it is ³⁄₈in (10mm).

12 Using a bowl gouge, round off the outer corner into a smooth curve (*see* Fig 10.13).

13 Sand and finish this side.

14 Using callipers and a pencil, re-mark the inner diameter (as before) that has since been lost due to cutting and sanding. It is important to ensure that the diameter exactly matches the circle on the other side. In this example, the inner diameter is 1in (25mm).

15 As before, cut a groove on the inside of this marked circle, but this time cut right through. At this point the outside ring will be cut free. To prevent it from becoming damaged by spinning against the tool rest it is a good idea to wrap a piece of soft cloth firmly around the tool rest to cushion the blow, should it spin off in that direction (making sure that there are no loose ends on the cloth that could become entangled).

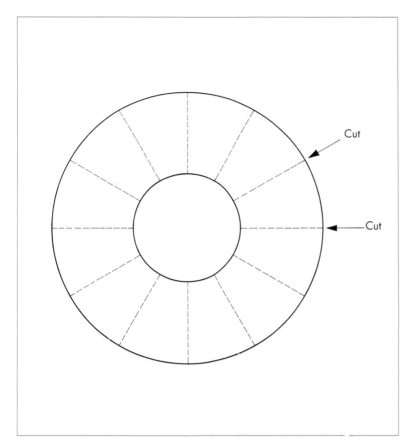

Fig 10.14 Cut along the line of each marked segment.

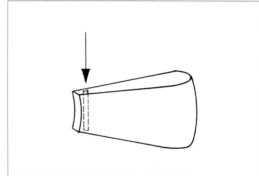

Side view

Fig 10.15 The finished bead.

Fig 10.16 Drilling the hole.

16 Remove the outer ring from the lathe. It is now ready to be cut into segments. Each segment becomes a 'bead' as follows:

17 Using a straightedge and a pencil, mark off a number of equidistant segments. Either eight or twelve is easiest, depending on the overall size of the ring and the desired size and shape of the beads (*see* Figs 10.14 and 10.15). In this example, twelve segments are used. Using a bandsaw, cut along the line of each marked segment.

18 Using a pillar drill, drill a small hole through the top sides of each bead, as shown in Fig 10.16.

19 Sand and finish the sides of each bead by hand, tidying up any rough edges.

The above method can be used with variations in the dimensions to produce beads of different widths and lengths.

Fig 10.17 Examples of long, flat beads made by the 'ring' method.

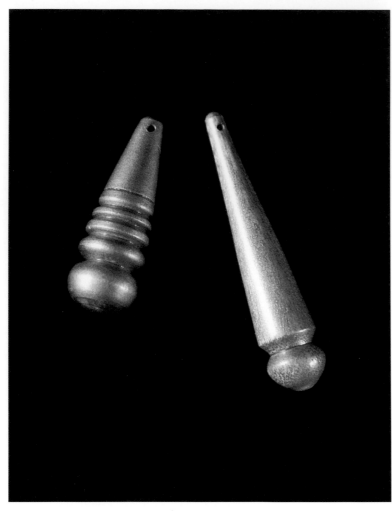

Fig 10.18 Examples of 'cylindrical' beads.

'CYLINDRICAL' BEADS

Strictly speaking these beads are not really cylindrical but more like elongated rain drops (*see* Fig 10.18). They are made in exactly the same way as the pendant earrings described in Chapter 6 (*see* pages 36–40), except that the hole is drilled horizontally across the top of the stem, not vertically downwards (*see* Fig 10.19). When strung together these beads can produce an attractive shape (*see* Fig 10.20).

Fig 10.20 A necklace made from cylindrical beads.

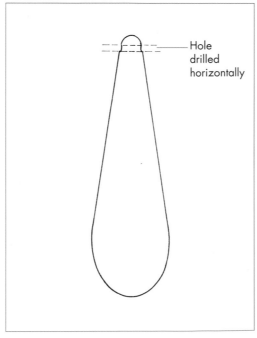

Fig 10.19 'Cylindrical' bead.

Hole
drilled
horizontally

THREADING UP

1 When all the beads have been turned, select a length of strong thread or cord, and thread the beads in the desired fashion. If you are using beads of different shapes and sizes it is a good idea to lay them all out in a line in the intended order, and with spacers where necessary, *before* threading them up. This helps to avoid mistakes.

2 When the threading is complete, check to see that the necklace is the right length. You may find that one or two beads need to be added or removed to achieve the length desired.

3 Finally, attach a clasp to the free ends of the thread.

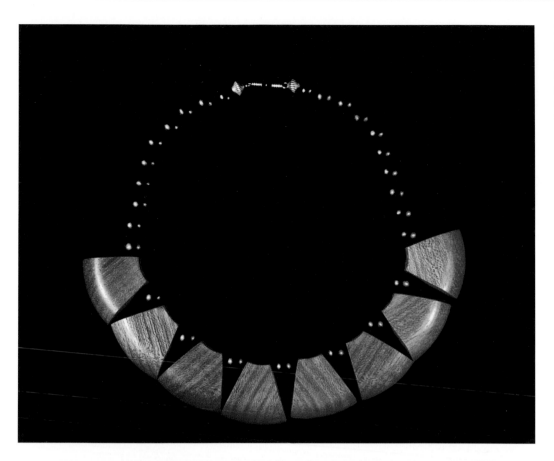

Fig 10.21 A necklace consisting of purple-heart beads made by the 'ring' method. The spacers are ordinary black wooden beads.

Fig 10.22 A necklace made from lignum-vitae beads stained with silk dye. The spacers are brass beads.

Fig 10.23 A necklace made from padauk and rosita beads. The spacers are ordinary small wooden beads.

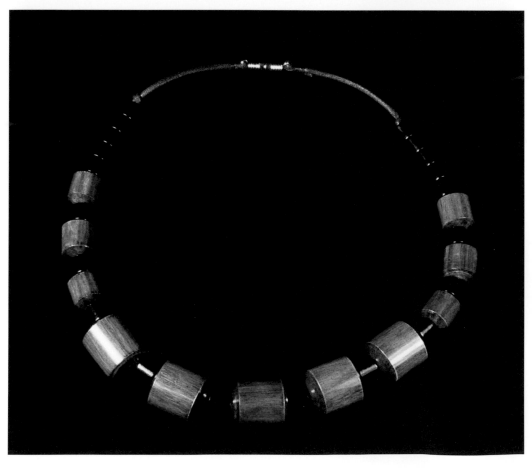

Fig 10.24 A necklace made from lignum-vitae beads stained with Liberon powder dye. The spacers are black wooden beads.

PART THREE

Further Techniques and Refinements

Stains and Dyes

Inlaying Wire

Laminating

Other Decorative Techniques

Finishing Techniques

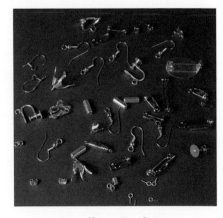

Jewellery Findings

Turning Alternative Materials

11

Stains and Dyes

▌ To colour or not to colour
▌ Selecting colours
▌ What are stains and dyes?
▌ Commercially produced stains and dyes

▌ The use of natural ingredients
▌ Points for consideration when staining wood
▌ The importance of experimentation

TO COLOUR OR
NOT TO COLOUR

INEVITABLY, THERE EXISTS in the turning world a controversy over whether wood should be coloured or whether it should always be left in its natural state. The purists argue that the natural colour of wood should be appreciated in its own right, and that using any form of colour is like 'gilding the lily'. Wood, they say, should look like wood and by colouring it we are making it look like something else, thereby devaluing it. Certainly, all people who choose to work with wood appreciate its natural beauty and there are many, many woods whose natural colours surpass anything that could be contrived by the hand of man. The natural colours and lustres that are revealed through the cutting and polishing processes can be seen as a celebration of nature's beauty.

The pragmatists, on the other hand, argue that while all the above may be true, there are in fact quite justifiable reasons for colouring wood. These reasons include the following:

1 Although there are some native timbers that have very attractive colours, the woods with the brightest and most interesting colours tend to be the exotic varieties imported from tropical rainforests. These are expensive to buy, and are in many cases under threat of extinction. For these reasons many people prefer not to buy them.

2 Some colourful varieties of wood may be hard to acquire, either because the nearest timber merchants have none in stock, or because they have none in the right dimensions, or because the only stockists might be at the other end of the country and to purchase through mail order would be too expensive. Many woodturners are aware of the necessity to buy certain varieties of timber when they are available, in the knowledge that the suppliers might be out of stock later when they really need it!

3 Some colours, especially blues and greens, simply do not occur in natural wood and must therefore be artificially applied if they are needed. This is often the case with jewellery, where items are often required to match certain articles of clothing, as accessories and so forth. Staining wood is therefore frequently an essential part of the process, especially where a particular shade is desired.

SELECTING COLOURS

Having said this, it is worth using wood's natural colour whenever possible. Apart from anything else, colouring wood can be messy and time consuming, and there is no point in embarking on it unless you feel it is necessary.

Another consideration is the nature of the dyes used. If wood is to be coloured at all, one should try to ensure that it still looks like wood afterwards. Therefore, avoid using anything opaque, such as paint, which will obscure the grain. The grain is, after all, one of the things which distinguishes wood from other materials, and to cover it up would be a waste of a highly decorative feature. Most turners would agree that it is in everyone's interests to bring to public attention the beauty and value of wood, and this will not be achieved by covering up the grain and making the wood look artificial. For these reasons, therefore, I would recommend that *transparent* dyes and stains are used for the most part. Of course, nothing is absolute in this field, and there are occasions when opaque colours *can* be used to good decorative effect, provided they are used sparingly. In the end, it is down to personal taste.

The shades of the colours chosen are also important. In order to avoid an artificial look, it is advisable to choose colours that at least look natural, even if they are not. For example, wood is not blue naturally, so try to create the sort of blue that wood might reasonably be if it were! This is not as easy as it sounds. Again, there are exceptions to every rule, and occasionally even colours that are clearly not natural-looking can nevertheless look very attractive.

WHAT ARE STAINS AND DYES?

Stains are usually differentiated from dyes in terms of the way they work. Dyes tend to be liquids containing particles of pigment, and these pigments are imparted permanently to the fibres of the wood. Stains, on the other hand, have a different mode of operation; in many cases they react with the host substance (in this case wood) to create a chemical reaction, which turns the wood a different colour. This rather oversimplifies the two processes, however it is unnecessary to examine the exact differences in detail. It is more useful to know what is available and how well it works.

Before embarking upon the process of dyeing and staining, it is important to understand that all the various commercially available products tend to fall into three distinct categories, depending upon their base. These are as follows:

WATER-BASED STAINS
Water-based stains are widely available from a number of manufacturers and their main advantage is that they are compatible with most finishes. Their disadvantage is that, because they are water based, they will raise the grain of the wood. In order to overcome this problem the surface of the wood must be wetted and sanded down with a fine grade of abrasive paper or cloth when dry, *before* applying the dye.

SPIRIT- OR ALCOHOL-BASED STAINS
These all have some form of alcohol as their base, and have the advantage of not raising the grain. Their disadvantage is that they are not recommended for use under spirit-based finishes such as sanding sealers or friction polishes, since these will tend to dissolve the dye.

However, this is not a hard-and-fast rule and there are ways round this problem. For example, if the dye solution applied to the wood is very dilute, a spirit-based finish *can* be used. Another option that sometimes works is to apply carefully and lightly an initial coat of spirit-based finish to the dyed wood surface, followed by a second coat after the first has dried. I have also heard that if a small amount of finish (e.g. sanding sealer) is added to the dye solution before applying it to the wood, this helps to seal the dye into the wood and makes the application of further finish satisfactory. In other words, it is possible to use finishes such as spirit-based sanding sealers on top of spirit-based dyes provided that only light coats of both are used, and are applied with care.

Another option is to apply several light coats of spray-on melamine. Alternatively, a water-based acrylic finish (which is a type of varnish) would be compatible with a spirit-based dye. (Varnishes tend to sit on top of the wood as opposed to sinking in.)

OIL-BASED STAINS
Like spirit-based stains and dyes, these have the advantage of not raising the wood grain; for similar reasons they are not recommended for use under oil-based finishes such as tung oil, or Danish oil, since these would tend to dissolve the dye.

It is also possible to colour wood using various chemical stains, such as ammonia, bichromate of potash, and so forth. However, these tend to work only on certain woods and the results can be unpredictable. Success with such chemicals therefore depends on much experimentation.

COMMERCIALLY PRODUCED STAINS AND DYES

There are many brands of commercially produced stains and dyes, and a few of the more common ones are considered below.

WOOD STAINS

Various companies produce wood stains, mainly targeted at woodwork enthusiasts who wish to create the effect of a certain type of wood. The colours tend to be labelled in terms of the wood shades that they claim to emulate; for example, mahogany, rosewood, yellow pine, etc. Anyone who has used these will know that these labels are often very misleading! For those people interested in making jewellery rather than furniture, such woodstains are of little use, since they usually only represent a range of browns, and they duplicate woods that are in any case most probably available to the average turner, at least in small quantities.

It is worth noting that most commercially produced wood stains available at DIY stores are actually oil-based stains, despite the fact that the manufacturers recommend that users clean their brushes with white spirit – which misleadingly suggests that they are spirit-based.

WOOD DYES

These too are made by various manufacturers, and are appearing increasingly on the market. The colours sometimes tend to be rather unnatural looking, and are in some cases quite garish. Wood dyes come in various forms depending on the manufacturer. Liberon produce a range of acrylic water-based dyes that have a white, chalky paste base. They come in a range of pastel colours, some of which look a little artificial. They are rather opaque and tend to fill the grain with a white deposit.

Liberon also produce a range of water-soluble dyes in powder form that are mixed with hot water to produce a transparent liquid concentrate that can be further diluted. These produce a good, clear dye and some of the colours are attractive (*see* Fig 11.1). They can also be mixed with each other.

Briwax produce a range of water-based dyes but they tend to be rather dilute, so several coats need to be applied. Also, the colours look artificial, in my opinion.

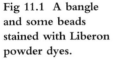

Fig 11.1 A bangle and some beads stained with Liberon powder dyes.

Fig 11.2

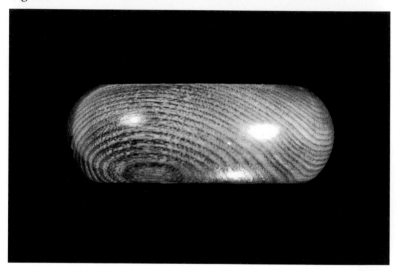

Fig 11.3

Figs 11.2 and 11.3 Bangles stained with aniline dyes. Both bangles have been stained with the same colour; the difference in appearance is because each was stained with a different concentration of the dye. The metallic effect was produced by a very concentrated dye solution.

Some of the spirit–soluble dyes produce quite pleasing colours, though some tend to go a little streaky.

ANILINE DYES

Anilines are alcohol-based compounds and have been used in dyeing since the mid-nineteenth century. Current manufacturers sometimes supply them in liquid form, which is most convenient but expensive. Other manufacturers (such as Mylands) supply them more cheaply in powder form and they then have to be mixed with

methylated spirit. They are versatile dyes, producing good strong colours that can be mixed with each other to produce a whole range of shades. They can be used in conjunction with any finish other than spirit-based ones. In concentrated form the dyes will often produce an attractive metallic effect (*see* Figs 11.2 and 11.3).

FABRIC DYES

These can be used very successfully on wood, and because most tend to be water based they can be used under any type of finish. There are many commercial brands to choose from with a huge range of intermixable colours. Some tend to be more opaque than others so it is worth experimenting with different brands. It is unwise to mix colours from different brands, however, because the colours often separate out.

SILK DYES

There is a wide range of silk dyes on the market, and they differ in terms of their opacity and colour range. Like fabric dyes, they work well on wood, and I can particularly recommend the Orient Express range. The colours in this range are rich and deep, and the dye itself is perfectly clear so there is no covering of the grain. Like ordinary fabric dyes, silk dyes also tend to be water based and can therefore be used under any finish. They also mix well (*see* Fig 11.4).

INKS

In general, coloured inks are not suitable for dyeing wood. They tend to be pale and the colours are not light-fast. The exception is Indian ink, which can be successfully used for staining wood black. This is expensive unless only small areas are to be stained. (Be sure to use the waterproof type.)

FOOD COLOURING

Commercial food colourings can also colour wood but they tend not to be light-fast so I would not recommend them.

Fig 11.5 A sycamore bangle stained with turmeric.

Fig 11.4 A bangle and some beads stained with silk dyes.

THE USE OF NATURAL INGREDIENTS

As an alternative to using commercial products it is also possible to stain wood using natural ingredients. There has been little research done in this area since the introduction of synthetic dyes, but I feel there are limitless possibilities here, particularly since, historically, dyeing was first carried out using only natural products.

TURMERIC

Having observed how a wooden spoon turns bright yellow after being used to stir curry, I was prompted to experiment with turmeric as a dye. This proved successful (*see* Fig 11.5) and the procedure is as follows:

Place a dessertspoon of turmeric powder into a small, non-stick saucepan and add approximately half a cup of water (the amounts are not critical). Add a small teaspoon of salt, bring to the boil and simmer gently for a few minutes until the solution turns an orange-brown colour. Apply to the wood after its surface has been wetted, left to dry and sanded. Apply two or three coats, depending on the intensity of colour required.

When dry, apply any finish. The colour produced is a bright lemon-yellow. The turmeric solution will keep for some time but not indefinitely.

ONION SKINS

A solution made from onion skins will produce a delightful warm orange colour. The procedure is as follows:

Remove the skins from three or four onions and boil them in water for about an hour until the solution turns a reddish-brown colour. Apply to the surface of the wood after it has been wetted and sanded. Several coats may be required (*see* Fig 11.6). The solution will keep for some time but not indefinitely.

Fig 11.6 An acacia bangle stained with onion skin.

NOTE 11.1 The readiness with which some woods react with water and iron to produce a black stain is also a reason for caution when using any water-based stain on wood. Never use wire wool for sanding prior to staining with a water-based stain. Microscopic particles of the wire wool (which is iron rich) will become embedded in the surface of the wood and these will often react with the water in the dye and the tannin in the wood to produce tiny spots of black stain.

There are undoubtedly many other similar possibilities, particularly with lichens and berries. It is worth being imaginative and above all willing to experiment.

TANNIN

Tannin is a chemical substance that exists in broad-leaved deciduous trees (hardwoods) to a variable degree. There are actually a number of tannins, differing from one another slightly in their chemical structure. Tannins are beneficial to the wood because, once harvested, they protect the wood from fungal attack.

Tannins are known for their use in tanning leather, where they react with skin proteins to cause a resistance to decay. This chemical behaviour of tannins also makes them useful in food processing, fruit ripening, and in the manufacture of coffee, tea and wine.

This may be of only passing interest to those concerned with staining wood, but of greater interest is the fact that the presence of tannin in wood can produce a deep black colour. Oak is perhaps the wood most widely-known to contain tannin, and many people will have observed the inky-black stains around old rusty nails that have been hammered into oak beams and posts. Iron, in the presence of water, will react chemically with the tannin, and the result of this is that the wood turns black.

This natural phenomenon is highly fortuitous for those of us who wish to achieve a good, deep, permanent black stain, although success will depend upon the type of wood. Some woods, such as oak and acacia, are rich in tannin and stain readily. Others contain relatively little tannin and cannot therefore be exploited in this way. Walnut and yew also contain moderate amounts of tannin. The easiest way of finding out whether a variety of wood is rich in tannin is to take an offcut and rub a wet piece of wire wool on the surface. Leave the wire wool in place overnight and inspect the wood the following day. The extent to which the wood has been stained black is an indication of the tannin content. The hue will also vary according to the wood. With oak, it is distinctly blue-black, whereas acacia produces a brown-black (*see* Fig 11.7). (*See* Note 11.1.)

The basic procedure for using the tannin content of wood to induce a black stain chemically is as follows:

When the item (preferably of oak) has had its final sanding, rub a piece of fine-grade wire wool dipped in water, back and forth across the surface with the lathe running. At first this will merely result in a faint grey colour, but if this is left to dry for a few minutes and the process is repeated several times, eventually a deep black colour will be obtained. This can be a slow process because the colour change is only gradual, so do not expect immediate results. The process is much quicker, however, if a solution of white vinegar and iron filings is used instead of water (*see* Fig 11.8). (Some people recommend a coating of oil on top to bring the colour to a full rich black, though I have not found this necessary and prefer to apply sanding sealer or melamine, but that is personal preference.) There is no need to raise and sand the grain before this process because, although the grain is raised by the water, the wire wool is continuously sanding it down, thus killing two birds with one stone.

Fig 11.7 An oak (left) and an acacia bangle stained with tannin.

Fig 11.8 Staining oak with a solution of iron filings and vinegar.

POINTS FOR CONSIDERATION WHEN STAINING WOOD

METHOD OF APPLICATION

It is usual to apply the stain or dye with a brush, though a cloth pad can be used. If you use brushes, be meticulous when you clean them, and if you intend to dye wood regularly, it is advisable to keep a set of brushes, one for each colour. It is very easy to *think* you have cleaned your brush thoroughly, but when you come to use it again with a different colour you may find that you have not! Even the slightest remaining trace of a previous dye will contaminate the new one.

SURFACE QUALITY

One of the most commonly held misconceptions about staining wood is that the stain will hide any blemishes or defects such as scratches on the surface of the wood. In fact, the reverse is true. Any scratches will

be magnified tenfold! This also applies to patches that have been insufficiently sanded, which will appear much darker than the rest of the wood once it is stained. With softer woods, where end grain can be difficult to sand, this can pose a problem. Consequently, do not attempt to stain anything until you are satisfied that the article has been thoroughly sanded with a fine grade of abrasive cloth. Since rough patches are more porous they absorb stain more readily than smooth areas, so it is essential to ensure that the surface quality is uniform throughout, otherwise the surface will look patchy. The finer the degree of sanding, the less the absorption, and the paler the colour.

DIFFERENTIAL ABSORPTION

End grain absorbs stain more readily than side grain, therefore the depth of hue will depend on which type of grain the dye has been applied to. Objects such as bangles, therefore, which have areas of side grain *and* end grain will vary in their depth of hue, depending on which part of the bangle is being observed. In fact, this is not a problem, and the constantly varying hue can look extremely attractive, particularly as the end grain and side grain also reflect light differently. It all adds to the appeal.

TEST SAMPLES

Always try out a stain or dye on a sample piece first, before applying it to the final article. It is important that the sample wood is of the same type as the object to be dyed, because different varieties of wood react differently to the same stain or dye. It is also important to ensure that your test sample has been sanded to the same degree as the intended final article, for the reasons mentioned above. Also, use the same concentration of dye. Unless all these variables are held constant there is no point in doing a test sample.

Test samples are also useful for discovering which types of finish are compatible with your dye and which are not.

You may be very aware that you should not use a spirit-based finish on top of a spirit-based dye, but quite often the manufacturers do not specify what the finish base is. Also, the degree of compatibility between a dye and a given finish does not always conform to neat rules and very often it will depend on the degree of concentration of the dye and other variables. So a trial-and-error method is sometimes inevitable.

Finally, let the stain dry thoroughly on your sample piece before coming to a decision about whether the colour is right. Dyed wood can look a completely different colour when wet than when it is dry.

BASE COLOUR

The colour of the base wood will affect the final colour. Whitish woods such as maple and holly are more likely to give a true colour, when dyed, than a darker wood, whose natural colour will affect the final colour of the dyed article. That is not to say that darker woods should not be dyed, but merely that they are less likely to produce a pure colour tone.

RECEPTIVITY

Some woods dye more easily than others. This can be due to their density, porosity, and degree of oiliness. Sycamore is particularly good to dye. It is pale in colour, sands easily, and readily absorbs dye. Acacia is also good and its attractive pattern of growth rings is enhanced through the dyeing process because of the differential absorption of the dense summer-wood and the more porous, less dense, spring-wood.

EFFECT OF FINISHES

Different finishes also have different effects on the final colour, so it is recommended that on your sample piece of wood you also apply the desired finish in order to judge the final result. Some finishes can alter the final colour quite markedly. Most finishes will darken the colour to a greater or lesser extent (*see* Chapter 15).

LIGHT-FASTNESS

Dyes and stains vary in their fastness to light. Some are extremely resilient to the effects of sunlight, while others fade quite rapidly. It is difficult to predict how well a given dye will stand the test of time, and the only sure way to find out is to leave a dyed item for several months and see how it fares. Generally speaking, most colours will fade if exposed to strong sunlight for long periods, so it is a good idea to keep finished items wrapped up or in a drawer away from light if you want them to retain their maximum strength of colour for a long period of time. (Of course, many undyed woods that start out with beautiful, vivid colours will gradually fade or turn more brown within a few months anyway.)

THE IMPORTANCE OF EXPERIMENTATION

The key to understanding staining and dyeing is to keep trying different methods all the time. Try different woods to find out which ones stain well and which do not. Try different stains and dyes to find out which colours are most suitable, and how they compare under different finishes. Try making your own dyes from natural ingredients and make a note of their light-fastness over a period of time. Keep your test samples and label them with the type of stain used, the dilution (if appropriate), the species of wood, the finish used, and the date. In this way you will gradually build up a useful bank of information for future reference. Another advantage of doing this is that if you are ever asked to produce an item of a particular shade and hue, it will be easier for you to select the right combination by referring to your bank of test samples. It may sound time consuming but it is something that can be gradually built up over time as you continue to experiment. Above all, *do* use your imagination, and experiment. Some of the most interesting effects can be produced by trying things that nobody else has thought of!

CHAPTER

12
Inlaying Wire

- ▌ Different types of wire
- ▌ Thickness of wire
- ▌ Basic procedure

- ▌ Spiral inlay
- ▌ Diagonal inlay
  on bangles

ESSENTIAL EQUIPMENT

- ▌ Lathe
- ▌ Basic turning tools
- ▌ Cyanoacrylate glue
- ▌ Wire
- ▌ Craft knife

RECOMMENDED EQUIPMENT

- ▌ Mini-hacksaw

LEVEL OF SKILL: Novice to intermediate

THE PROCESS OF INLAYING wire is a useful decorative technique, which can enhance the appearance of a wide variety of objects, including jewellery. Once mastered, it is a fairly straightforward procedure which need not take too long, and the extra bit of time is well spent since it can turn an otherwise ordinary piece into something special.

DIFFERENT TYPES OF WIRE

Perhaps the most common types of wire to use for inlay are silver, copper and brass. These are also probably the most easy to obtain, but if you have access to any other types it is worth experimenting. Pewter would probably work well, and also gold, if you can afford it!

Silver wire can be obtained from certain hobby and craft shops, but be careful because sometimes the wire is actually silver–plated copper (the price should give you some indication). Silver wire can also be bought in some jewellery shops where jewellery is made on the premises. It is normally sold by weight, and an obliging jeweller will 'draw' it down to any thickness you wish.

Copper and brass wire can be found in a variety of places. Some hardware stores sell it, and it can sometimes be found in electrical shops and DIY stores. Scrap metal merchants are also worth trying. It is worth

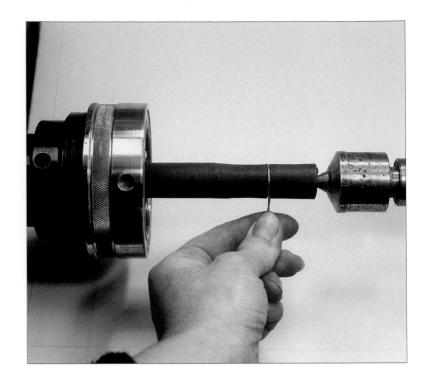

keeping a lookout wherever you happen to be because it is exactly the sort of thing that is frequently thrown away, often as part of some other piece of junk. After all, if you can get it for next to nothing, why buy it new?

THICKNESS OF WIRE

To a certain extent this will depend on the size of the object. Small items such as earrings will need a thinner wire than larger items such as bangles, though thin wire can also be used effectively on large objects.

Fig 12.1 Check that the wire fits the groove.

Fig 12.2 The shape of the groove is very important.

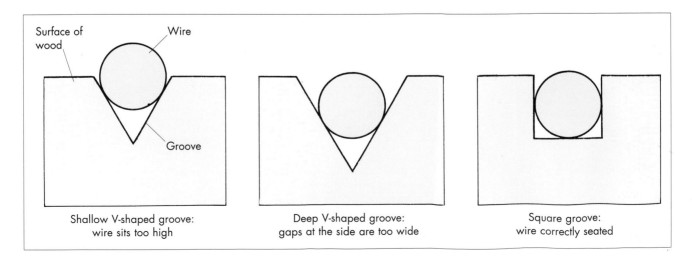

Surface of wood   Wire

Groove

Shallow V-shaped groove:
wire sits too high

Deep V-shaped groove:
gaps at the side are too wide

Square groove:
wire correctly seated

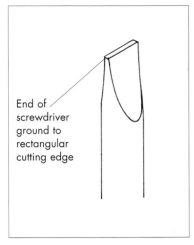

Fig 12.3 An adapted screwdriver.

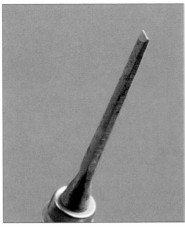

Fig 12.4 The screwdriver is ground to a flat, straight edge.

Basic Procedure

1 Turn the item to be inlaid to the desired size and shape. Some preliminary sanding may be done at this stage but it is not worth doing the final sanding because this will be done later when the wire has been embedded.

2 Having decided the exact position of the intended inlay, switch on the lathe and make a *small* groove with a sharp parting tool held sideways, i.e. with the cutting edge vertical.

3 Now extend this groove until it is the correct depth and width for the wire. (*See* Note 12.1.)

The thickness of wire that I find most useful is 0.0315in (0.8mm), as it is suitable for most items. Wire of 0.0236in (0.6mm) thickness is also satisfactory, but with wire this thin there is the risk of over-sanding and actually wearing the wire away in one or two places, obliging you to start again. It is therefore easier (unless you are quite skilled) to use thicker wire (e.g. 0.0315in [0.8mm]), since this gives you a wider margin of error. Wire thicker than 0.0315in (0.8mm) can also be used but it does tend to become less pliable as it gets thicker. It is also unsuitable for small items such as thin-stemmed earrings because the groove that has to be cut to receive the wire would need to be quite deep and would weaken the structure. Wire of 0.0394in (1mm) thickness is the thickest that I would use.

Fig 12.5 Cutting the groove.

NOTE 12.1 This stage is crucial. It is easy enough to achieve the correct width and this can be tested at intervals to see if the wire fits the groove (*see* Fig 12.1). However, the *shape* and the *depth* of the groove are critical. The cross section of the groove should be square (not V shaped) so that the wire lies in it correctly (*see* Fig 12.2), and this cannot be achieved with a parting tool alone. I have adapted an old screwdriver by grinding the end straight across to produce a cutting tool of the appropriate width and shape (*see* Figs 12.3, 12.4 and 12.5). This is an important step because, as Fig 12.2 shows, a V-shaped groove will not allow the wire to embed itself correctly. Either the wire will sit too high on the surface of the wood or, if the groove is deeper, the gaps on either side will be too wide at the surface.

The depth of the groove is also critical. If the wire is not set deeply enough too much of its width will lie proud of the surface and will eventually be sanded away, causing a break in the line. If it is set too deeply, much sanding is required to produce a continuous flat edge (*see* Fig 12.6). It is safer, though, to set the wire too deep rather than too shallow because it is easier to sand it down than to start all over again because of a break in the line. The correct depth for the wire is roughly level with the surface of the wood, or just very slightly higher. At this depth, after sanding, the wire will be flattened evenly without removing too much of its width, or too much of the surrounding wood. Clearly, the thicker the wire, the deeper the groove will need to be in order to accommodate it. The narrower the wire, the more critical is the depth of groove because narrower wire is more readily sanded away.

It does not matter if the width of the groove is *slightly* too wide. This will not result in a gap either side, because during sanding the malleable property of the wire enables it to spread to fill the gap. This is why, after sanding, the wire appears slightly wider than its original thickness.

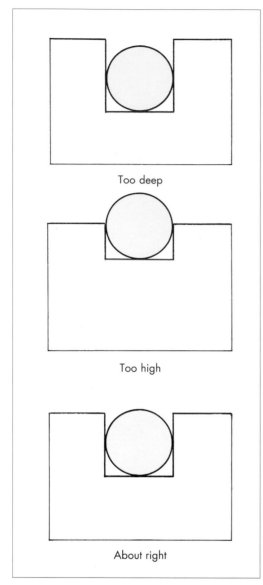

Fig 12.6 **The depth of the groove is critical.**

(Too deep)

(Too high)

(About right)

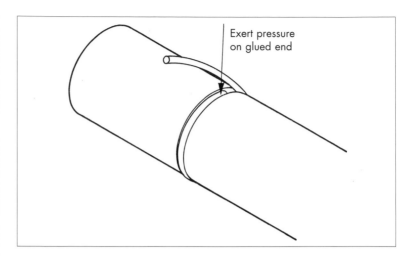

Exert pressure
on glued end

Fig 12.7 **Wrap
the wire around
the wood.**

4 When you are satisfied that the proportions of the groove are correct, check once again by placing a length of wire in it to see if it fits snugly. However, do not at this stage cut it to the right length.

5 Trickle cyanoacrylate glue into the groove. A non-viscous variety usually works well since it will run along the length of the groove, filling it quite quickly. (*See* Note 12.2.)

6 Now place one end of the wire in the groove and wrap the rest of the wire around, pulling it taut so that the groove is filled for most of its length (*see* Fig 12.7). It is important that the wire is pulled taut so that it is bedded down as deep as it will go.

NOTE 12.2 It is worth experimenting with different varieties of such glue because some types seem to work much more effectively than others. It you find there is a problem getting the wire to adhere to the wood, it is possibly because the glue you have chosen is not the best type for the job. Loctite superglue works well.

Fig 12.8 **Hold the
wire in place until
the glue has set.**

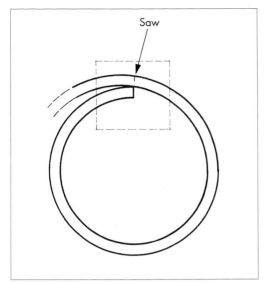

Fig 12.9

Figs 12.9 and 12.10 **Saw part way through with a sharp blade.**

Fig 12.10

7 Hold the wire in place until the glue has fully set. An old pair of small pliers is ideal for this job (*see* Fig 12.8).

8 When the glue has set, the wire will be securely embedded and attention can now be given to finishing off the free end.

Pull the free end of the wire around so that it rests on top of the glued end. With a sharp craft knife blade, saw a little way through the free end of the wire at precisely the point above contact with other end (*see* Figs 12.9 and 12.10). Do not attempt to saw through completely or you will run the risk of damaging the surface of the wood.

9 Holding the wire firmly at its point of contact in the groove, move the free end backwards and forwards until it breaks off in the position of the saw cut (*see* Fig 12.11). If necessary, this broken end can be filed to a flat edge (*see* Fig 12.12).

10 With the addition of a bit more glue, the free end can now be embedded and held securely until the glue has set (*see* Fig 12.13). If the procedure has succeeded, the join will only just be visible (*see* Figs 12.14 and 12.15).

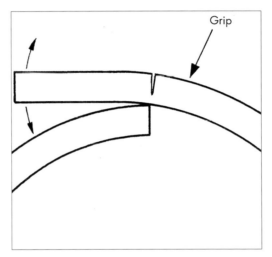

Fig 12.11 **Move the free end up and down until it breaks off.**

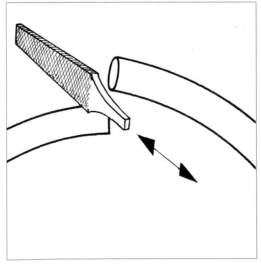

Fig 12.12 **File the end flat.**

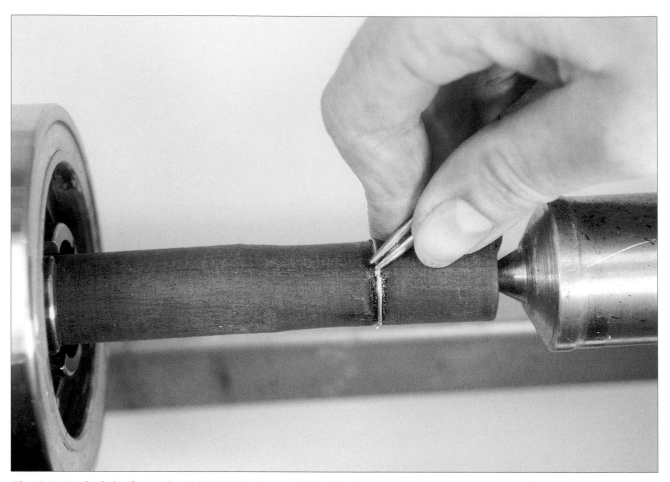

Fig 12.13 Embed the free end and hold it in place until the glue has set.

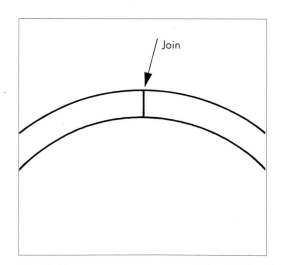

Join

Fig 12.14

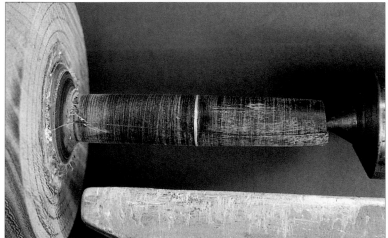

Figs 12.14 and 12.15 The join should barely be visible.

Fig 12.15

11 Sand with an abrasive no coarser than 180 grit and work down the grades in the normal way. The wire will be flattened out through sanding and it is important to ensure that this flattening is even and has occurred right around the ring of wire.

12 Apply the desired finish to the whole item in the usual way.

The above technique can be used to inlay wire in any size of object, from narrow earrings to broad bangles.

SPIRAL INLAYS

It is also possible to inlay wire in a spiral fashion, though the process takes longer. Although the general principles are the same, the technique of making the groove is rather different. It is a process mainly suitable for long, thin items such as earrings, for example. The method is described below:

1 Turn the object intended for inlay to its final shape, leaving some excess wood at each end (which will later be removed), but do not do the final sanding at this stage. With the item supported between centres on a stationary lathe, saw a groove with a small hacksaw in a diagonal line across the wood, slowly rotating it by hand as you go (*see* Fig 12.16). (The hacksaw blade should be wide enough to produce a groove of sufficient width to accommodate the wire.) Extreme care is needed at this stage to avoid damaging the wood on either side of the line of cut. As you rotate the wood, *keep the angle of cut constant.* When you reach the other end, return to the beginning and repeat the process until the groove is the correct depth. Care must be taken to ensure that the cut groove is exactly the same depth all the way along its length. Failure to do so will result in uneven bedding of the wire.

2 Trickle glue along the length of the groove as described previously (*see* page 94). If the item is fairly large it is wise to apply glue to only part of its length at a time.

3 Beginning at one end, place one end of the wire in the groove and hold it securely as before, while slowly embedding the rest of it along the groove. This may need to be done in stages, depending on the length of the area to be covered. Grip the wire in place until the glue has set.

4 Sand as before.

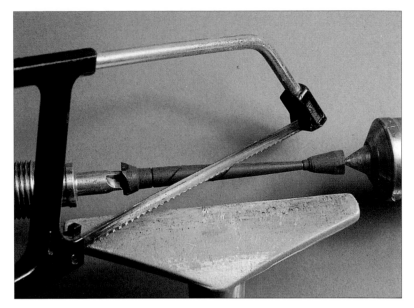

Fig 12.16 A diagonal groove being cut in an earring.

Fig 12.17 The finished ebony earrings with spiral inlay.

5 Switch on the lathe and finish turning the ends of the item, removing the excess wood. You will find that you cut through the ends of the wire, but provided it has been securely glued, this does not matter.

6 Apply the desired finish in the usual way.

DIAGONAL INLAYS ON BANGLES

It is also possible to inlay wire in equidistant diagonal lines on bangles (*see* Fig 12.18). This can look extremely effective. The method is described below:

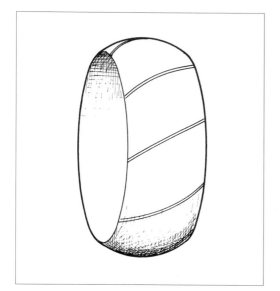

Fig 12.18 A bangle with diagonal inlays.

1 Turn the bangle to the desired shape but do not do the final sanding at this stage.

2 With the bangle secured on the stationary lathe, mark out along one edge a series of equidistant dots. In order to do this you will need to calculate the circumference by using

the formula 2πr, where π = 3.142 and r = the radius of the rim of the bangle. For example, with a rim of radius 35mm (1⅜in), the circumference would be 2 x 3.142 x 35. This works out at approximately 220mm (8¹⁄₁₆in). Divide this number by the number of diagonal inlays you wish to make. For example, if 7 inlays were desired; then 220 ÷ 7 = 31mm (1¼in) So, 7 inlays would have a distance of 31mm (1¼in) between each one, and you would therefore mark the dots at intervals of this distance along the rim (*see* Fig 12.19). (*See* Note 12.3.)

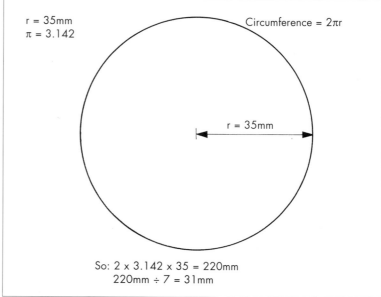

$$r = 35mm$$
$$\pi = 3.142$$

Circumference = 2πr

r = 35mm

So: 2 x 3.142 x 35 = 220mm
220mm ÷ 7 = 31mm

Fig 12.19 Calculating the circumference of a circle, and then subdividing into seven equal parts.

Fig 12.20   **Figs 12.20 and 12.21 Find the radius and mark off six arcs around the circumference with a   Fig 12.21
pair of compasses. (The marks have been overemphasized for clarity within the photo.)**

NOTE 12.3 There is an easier method of subdividing the circumference, which results in six inlays: Find the radius of the rim and set a pair of compasses to this distance. Beginning at any point on the rim, mark off a series of arcs all the way round. This will result in six equidistant points along the rim (*see* Figs 12.20 and 12.21). This only works for six points, but a further subdivision of these points could give twelve inlays.

3 Now decide the angle of the desired diagonal for the inlays. This can be done by stretching a piece of string from one of the dots diagonally across the width of the bangle to the opposite rim (*see* Fig 12.22). Adjust the position of the string until the desired angle is obtained.

4 Mark the spot where the string meets the opposite rim.

5 Starting from this spot, mark out the remaining dots in exactly the same way as on the previous side, at the same distance apart.

6 Now you are ready to start cutting the grooves. Using a hacksaw in the manner previously described (*see* page 97), make diagonal saw cuts from a dot on the side of one rim across to its diagonal partner on the other rim. In other words, follow the same line as the string (*see* Fig 12.23).

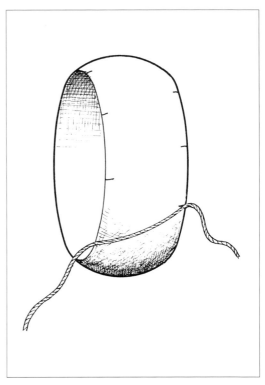

Fig 12.22 Stretch a piece of string across from one side to the other at the desired angle.

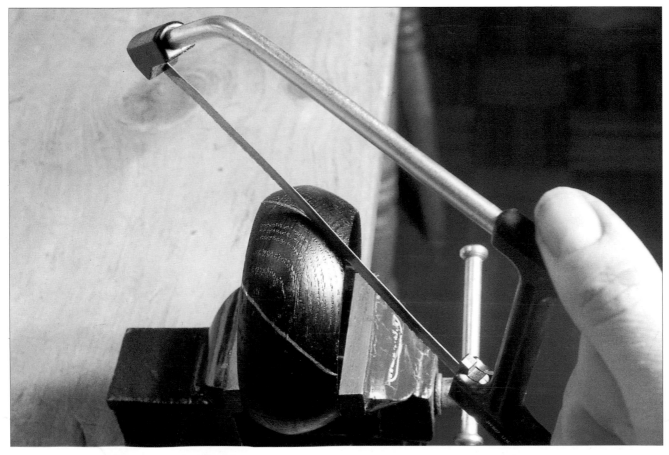

Fig 12.23 Making diagonal cuts in a bangle.

NOTE 12.4 When the wire has been glued into position and sanded, it can be polished to a high gloss using an ordinary metal polish. (This is best done just prior to applying the sealing finish.) This considerably improves the overall appearance and is worth doing where a dark wood such as ebony has been used. With lighter-coloured woods it is inadvisable because you run the risk of discolouring the wood in the process.

Fig 12.24 A stained oak bangle with silver wire diagonally inlaid.

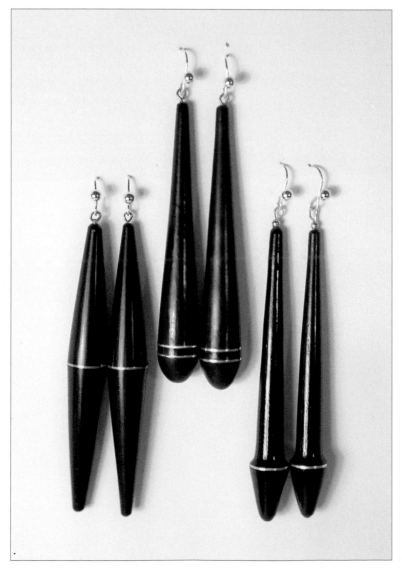

7 When the groove has been satisfactorily cut, proceed to the next dot and repeat the process until all the grooves have been cut. Once again, ensure that the grooves are of the correct width and depth all the way along their length.

8 Embed the wire in the manner previously described (*see* pages 94–95).

9 Sand and finish in the usual way.

With further experimentation, other variations on the same theme may be found.

See Note 12.4.

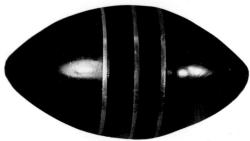

Fig 12.25 Ebony earrings with various kinds of inlaid wire, including copper and brass.

Fig 12.26 An oval, side-grain, ebony brooch with inlaid silver wire.

13

Laminating

- Initial preparations
- Longitudinal stripes
- Lateral stripes
- Diagonal stripes
- Laminates of unequal width
- Using more than two contrasting timbers
- Laminated blanks for bangles
- Coopering
- Laminating with sheet metal
- Some final thoughts on laminating

ESSENTIAL EQUIPMENT

- Bandsaw
- Strong glue
- Cramps (various)

LEVEL OF SKILL: Intermediate

L AMINATING is the process of bonding together thin layers of material. In this chapter we will be looking at bonding thin layers of different-coloured woods into composite striped blocks (or blanks) which can then be used in a variety of ways.

The preparation of small laminated blanks (e.g. for earrings) and larger blanks (e.g. for bangles) is also described. There is a description of the related technique of coopering, which is useful for preparing laminated bangle blanks. It should be pointed out at this stage that access to a bandsaw is absolutely essential for making the laminates.

The purpose of laminating is to produce an attractive effect through the use of contrasting colours. Before starting, a number of decisions will need to be made regarding the nature of the finished composite block, namely:

HOW MANY DIFFERENT TYPES OF WOOD ARE TO BE USED?

It is a good idea, when beginning, to start off with just two. In any case, keeping to two colours can often give a better and more striking effect than if more colours are used. But this is a matter of personal choice.

WHICH WOODS ARE TO BE USED?

Bearing in mind the guidelines given in Chapter 3, this is also a matter of personal choice, though it is advisable to select timbers of contrasting colours, preferably matching dark with light. Remember also that timbers that may look quite different in large blocks often appear very similar when laminated, which reduces the impact of the stripes, so aim for as much contrast as possible.

Try to avoid timbers that already have a pronounced figure, such as stripes or bands or a strong grain pattern. Such timbers are better kept for use on their own, since they can reduce the visual impact of the laminating. Choose fairly hard, plain, fine-grained woods, if possible. Good examples are sycamore, maple, holly, amarello, purple heart and padauk. There are, of course, many others.

WHAT WIDTH SHOULD THE STRIPES BE?

This will depend on the ultimate size and shape of the object to be made, and also upon the desired visual effect.

IN WHICH DIRECTION SHOULD THE STRIPES RUN?

They can be longitudinal (*see* Fig 13.1), lateral (*see* Fig 13.2), or diagonal (*see* Fig 13.3). Again, the choice will depend on the desired visual effect.

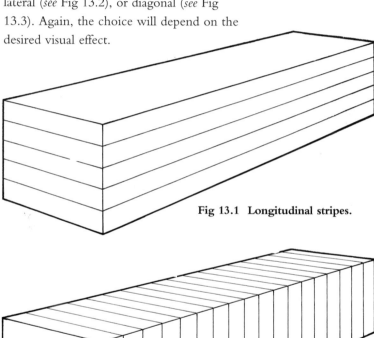

Fig 13.1 **Longitudinal stripes.**

Fig 13.2 **Lateral stripes.**

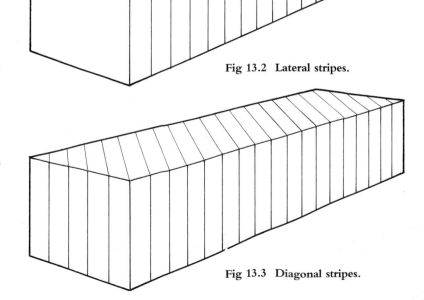

Fig 13.3 **Diagonal stripes.**

WHICH WAY SHOULD THE GRAIN RUN?

This is a technical rather than aesthetic decision. For faceplate turning, it is not a crucial factor, although it is usual to have the grain running at right angles to the bed. However, for between-centres or spindle turning, it is better to have the grain running parallel to the bed.

When the above decisions have been made, you are ready to start. To begin with, we will consider three different methods of producing stripes of equal width, using two contrasting woods. The longitudinal, lateral, and diagonal methods of laminating are each described in turn below.

INITIAL PREPARATIONS (APPLYING TO ALL THREE METHODS)

Having selected the two pieces of wood to be used, make sure they are both of square cross section and the same size. Between 1⁹⁄₁₆ and 1¹⁵⁄₁₆in (40 and 50mm) square is a useful size since the resulting block is large enough to be used for a variety of items. The dimensions will, of course, depend on the intended size and number of the finished items, and the length of each block of wood will depend upon how many laminates are required. About 7⅞in (200mm) might be a useful length to begin with. The selected pieces of wood can be cut and trimmed on a bandsaw to bring them to the correct size. There is always some wastage with laminating so you may prefer to use inexpensive timbers, at least to start with.

The following procedures are less time-consuming than they seem. And remember, if you begin with blocks of wood of a reasonable size you will end up with laminated blanks large enough to convert into many pieces of jewellery. For a more economic usage of time, put aside a period for preparation of laminated blanks for future use. That way you will never run out.

Fig 13.4 Making a longitudinal cut with the bandsaw.

LONGITUDINAL STRIPES

1 Having selected and prepared your two lengths of wood, position the rip fence on the bandsaw to give the desired width of cut and pass the first block through the bandsaw blade lengthwise (*see* Fig 13.4). This will give a long, narrow laminate (*see* Fig 13.5). While passing the wood through the blade, be careful not to press the wood too hard against the rip fence, and make sure that equal pressure is exerted on the leading and trailing edges. Failure to do so can result in a crooked cut and the machine becoming jammed. Take it slowly and gently. If there is a difficulty with the cut, check that the blade is sharp. A blunt blade will not do the job. If you are not able to produce laminates of consistently even thickness using your bandsaw, a planer-thicknesser is recommended.

2 Repeat this until you have sliced through the whole block.

3 Repeat with the second block.

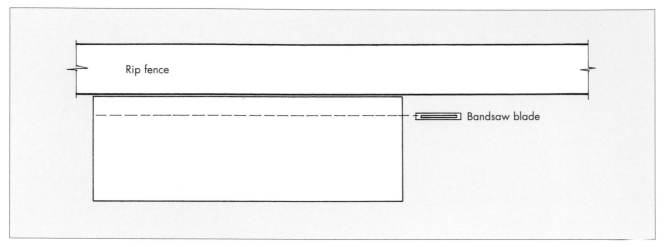

Fig 13.5 A block passed lengthwise through the bandsaw.

4 You should now have two piles of long laminates, one of each colour. Using a strong glue (e.g. Cascamite), stick the laminates together lengthwise, alternating the colours. Before gluing, examine the surfaces of the laminates. They may need some sanding to render them perfectly flat.

5 Cramp the block of laminates in a vice. Do not attempt to cramp the laminates while the glue is still very wet since they are likely to slide out of alignment. It is better to wait until the glue has begun to harden slightly before cramping. You will now have a laminated block with stripes running lengthwise (*see* Figs 13.6 and 13.7).

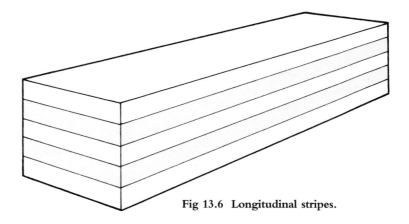

Fig 13.6 Longitudinal stripes.

6 When the joints are dry, trim the edges with a bandsaw and proceed to use your laminated blank as desired.

Fig 13.7 Longitudinal laminates glued and cramped up.

LATERAL STRIPES

There are two methods for this. The first results in a laminated blank with grain running parallel to the axis, which is preferable for spindle turning. The second produces a blank with the grain running at right angles, which is more suited to faceplate turning.

METHOD ONE (FOR GRAIN PARALLEL TO AXIS)

1 Stick the two selected pieces of wood together lengthwise with double-sided Sellotape, making sure that the ends are aligned.

Fig 13.8 Making lateral cuts with the bandsaw.

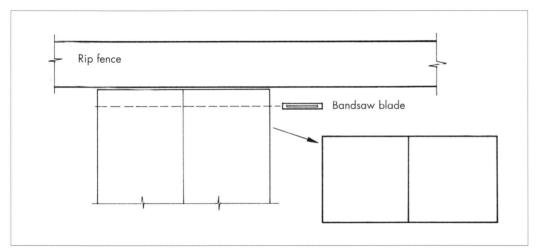

Fig 13.9 A double block being passed horizontally through the bandsaw.

Fig 13.10 Laminates glued to form lateral stripes.

2 Having decided on the desired width of the stripes (laminates), adjust the rip fence on the bandsaw to give the appropriate width of cut (¹⁄₁₆-¹⁄₈in [2-3mm] is about right).

3 Pass the double block of wood through the bandsaw blade repeatedly to produce a series of even slices (*see* Fig 13.8). Since the two pieces of wood are joined together you will obtain a 'double slice' each time the block is passed through (*see* Fig 13.9).

4 When you have reached the end of the wood you should have a pile of square laminates. Stick these together, as before, alternating the colours (*see* Fig 13.10).

Do not try to stick too many together at once. It is much easier to glue the laminates into smaller piles first and then glue these piles together afterwards when the first layers have dried.

5 By gluing the smaller piles into longer ones in this way you will end up with a very rough-looking rectangle of striped wood. You may find that there are a few gaps here and there along the length. These often occur due to the laminates bending (caused partly by the moisture in the glue). These gaps, provided they are not too big, can be filled with gap-filling superglue. (*See* Note 13.1.)

NOTE 13.1 Before filling small cracks with superglue, always rub the surface of the surrounding wood with some of the finish you intend to use (e.g sanding sealer or melamine). This prevents the surface of the wood becoming stained by the glue.

NOTE 13.2 The method described here results in end grain being glued. Although the joints will not be quite as strong as when gluing side grain, the advantage is that the resulting blank, when mounted between centres, will have all the grain running parallel to the bed, as in normal spindle turning. However, if this is not a necessary consideration, an alternative method of constructing the blanks is described in Method Two.

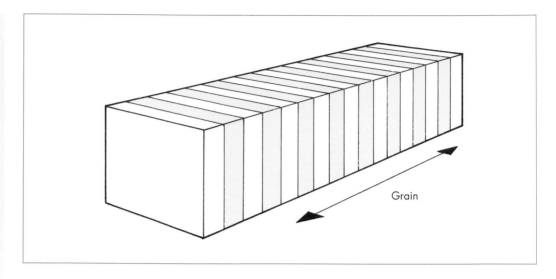

Fig 13.11 Lateral stripes with the grain running parallel to the axis.

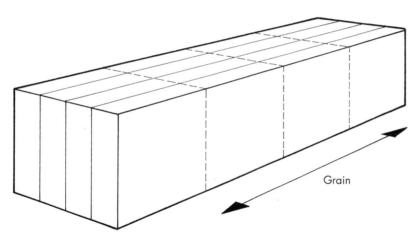

Fig 13.12 Laminates cut and glued lengthwise, then cut into cubes.

6 When all the joints are dry, trim the edges with the bandsaw. Your laminated blank is now ready to be converted into your chosen pieces of jewellery (*see* Fig 13.11). If small items are to be made, you will need to saw your blank further.

See Note 13.2.

METHOD TWO (FOR GRAIN AT RIGHT ANGLES TO AXIS)

1 Make longitudinal cuts with the bandsaw along the length of each block in turn, producing long, rectangular slices, following the instructions for longitudinal stripes (see pages 103–104).

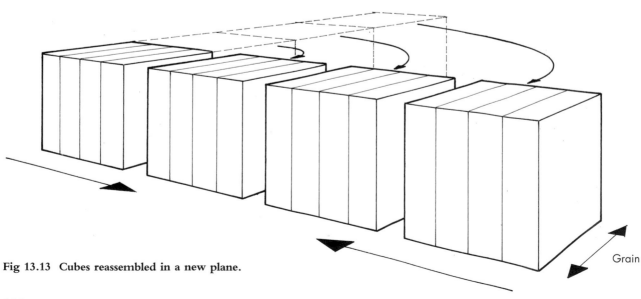

Fig 13.13 Cubes reassembled in a new plane.

2 Glue these side to side with the colours alternating.

3 Cut the resulting composite blocks laterally to produce cubes, and glue these together as shown in Figs 13.12–13.14 to produce a rectangular blank. The final blank will now have the grain running across, rather than along, its length. Such blanks would be suitable for faceplate turning, for example.

DIAGONAL STRIPES

This method is very similar to that for making lateral stripes.

1 Glue your two blocks of wood together lengthwise with double-sided Sellotape as previously described, but this time the ends should not be aligned. Offset one end approximately ¾–1¼in (20–30mm) below the other (*see* Fig 13.15). The 'offset distance' determines the angle of the stripes. The greater the offset distance, the steeper the angle of the stripe (and the more wastage of wood at each end). Therefore it is important

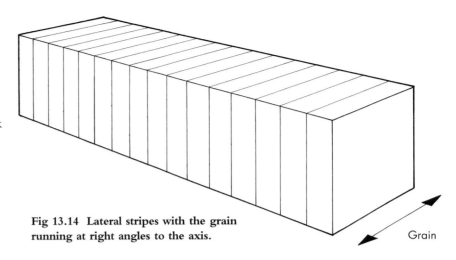

Fig 13.14 Lateral stripes with the grain running at right angles to the axis.

Grain

at this stage to decide roughly what angle of stripes you want.

The angle of the stripes will also depend upon the cross-sectional measurements of your selected blocks. For example, if your blocks are 2in (50mm) square, and the offset distance is 2in (50mm), this will produce a diagonal stripe of 45° (*see* Fig 13.16). If this is what you want, fine, but personally I find this angle unnecessarily steep and rather wasteful of wood. I prefer an angle of about 30°, which means that the offset distance should be approximately two-thirds of the

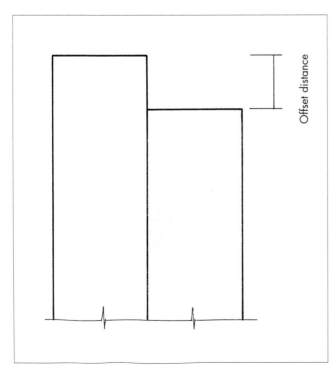

Fig 13.15 The blocks offset at the ends.

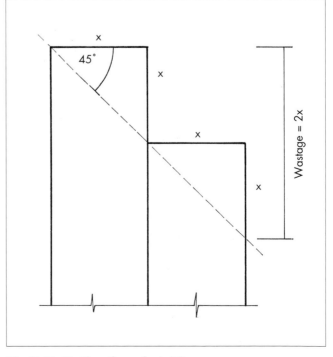

Fig 13.16 Cutting through at 45°.

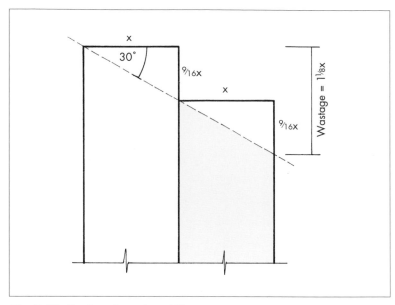

Fig 13.17 Cutting through at 30°.

cross-sectional measurement (*see* Fig 13.17). For example, if your blocks measure 2⅜in x 2⅜in (60mm x 60mm), then the offset distance should be somewhere in the region of 1⁹⁄₁₆in (40mm). However, these proportions need only be very approximate.

2 Place the double block on the bandsaw at the appropriate angle and make the first cut, which saws off the corners (*see* Figs 13.18 and 13.19).

3 Adjust the rip fence to the correct position for the desired width of cut and pass the block through the blade as previously described, keeping the blocks at the same angle (*see* Figs 13.20 and 13.21).

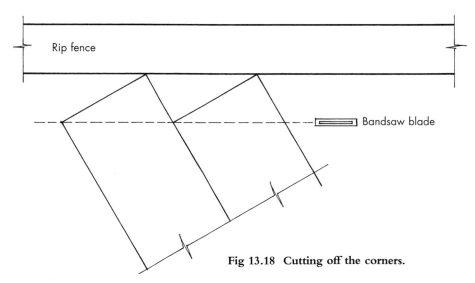

Fig 13.18 Cutting off the corners.

Fig 13.19 Making the initial diagonal cut with the bandsaw to remove the corners.

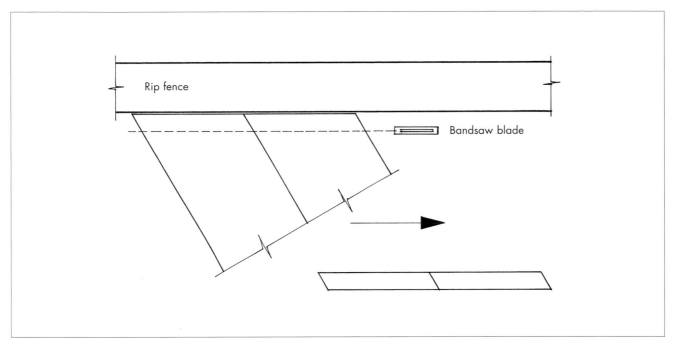

Fig 13.20 A double slice at 30°.

Fig 13.21 Making a double cut on the bandsaw.

4 Continue to repeat this until no more slices can be obtained. There will be some wastage of corners at the other end also.

5 Each laminate will have two edges that are sloping. It will also be slightly rectangular, rather than exactly square. Glue small piles of laminates together, as described in the section on lateral stripes, but make sure they are joined together so their edges follow the angle of slope (*see* Fig 13.22). This will result in small blocks with diagonal stripes (*see* Fig 13.23). When the joints are dry, glue together the small piles to form longer ones, as described in the previous section, and square off the ends (*see* Fig 13.24). Trim the edges on the bandsaw and the laminated blank is then ready for use (*see* Fig 13.25). Fig 13.26 shows finished earrings with diagonal stripes.

See Note 13.3.

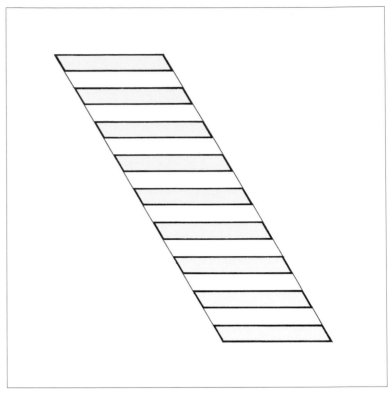

Fig 13.22 Laminates cut at 30° and assembled at an angle.

NOTE 13.3 If preferred, there is an alternative method of producing diagonal stripes, which does not involve making diagonal cuts on the bandsaw. Cut square slices as described in Method One for lateral stripes (*see* page 105), then glue these together in a slanting fashion (*see* Fig 13.27). A disadvantage with this is that the edges of the slices are not angled to give a guide for the angle of assembly when gluing up. Also, the resulting cross section will be somewhat smaller than that of the original blocks of wood, so this must be allowed for when selecting the original pieces.

Fig 13.23 Diagonal laminates glued up.

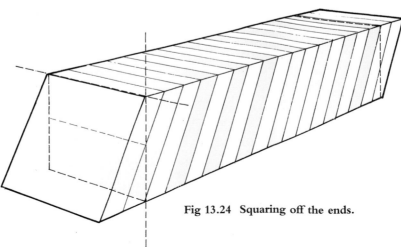

Fig 13.24 Squaring off the ends.

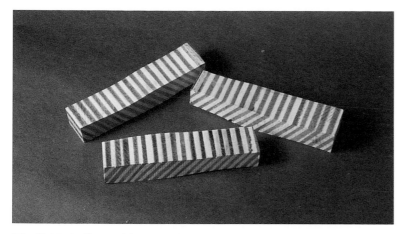

Fig 13.25 A diagonal laminate block sawn up into smaller blanks.

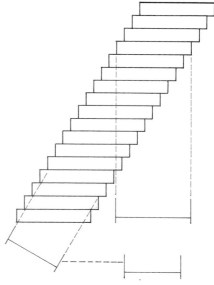

Fig 13.27 Laminates cut at 90°, and assembled at an angle.

Fig 13.26 Finished earrings of sycamore, purple heart and blackwood, made from diagonal laminates.

LAMINATES OF UNEQUAL WIDTH

The four methods described above all produce stripes of equal width. A slightly different effect can be created by using laminates of different widths, where one timber has much thinner bands than those of its contrasting partner (*see* Fig 13.28).

The methods for producing these are basically the same as those described previously, except that the rip fence must be positioned differently for one of the woods in order to produce a different thickness of laminate. Therefore, if horizontal or diagonal stripes are required, the two original woodblocks must be cut separately, not simultaneously, as described in the above methods.

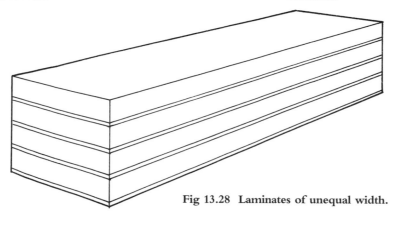

Fig 13.28 Laminates of unequal width.

USING MORE THAN TWO CONTRASTING TIMBERS

There is no limit to the number of different woods that can be used together and some very interesting effects can be created (*see* Fig 13.29). Even plywood (itself a laminate) can be used either on its own or in conjunction with other woods, though most types of plywood tend to be very soft and are therefore unsuitable. Hardwood ply, made from birch for example, is quite satisfactory and turns well, though it can be difficult to obtain.

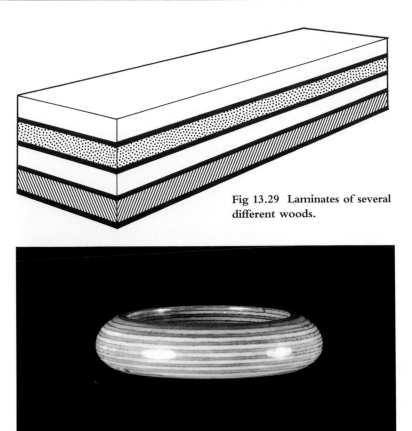

Fig 13.29 Laminates of several different woods.

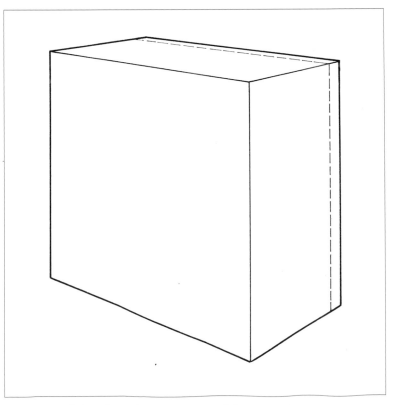

Fig 13.30 A bangle turned from birch plywood.

LAMINATED BLANKS FOR BANGLES

The above methods can be used to produce fairly small blanks with a small cross section, suitable for items such as earrings, brooches, beads, etc. It is, of course, possible to employ the same principles to produce blanks for bangles. There are a number of ways in which this can be done, depending on the desired direction of stripe:

LONGITUDINAL STRIPES

As before, decide how many different woods are to be used and in what combination.

1 Using the bandsaw, begin with two or more blocks of about 4in (100mm) square – the depth will depend upon the desired width of the bangle and the number of layers. Pass these through the bandsaw lengthwise (*see* Fig 13.31) to produce laminates of the desired width. Assemble in the desired fashion, glue, cramp, and leave to dry (*see* Fig 13.32).

Fig 13.31 Slicing through a block (in upright position) to produce square slices.

**Fig 13.32
Longitudinal
laminates glued and
cramped up ready
for a bangle blank.**

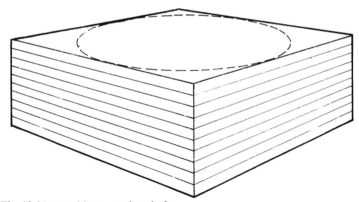

Fig 13.33 Marking out the circle.

2 Find the centre of one face and, using a
pair of compasses, draw a circle on the face
as large as possible.

3 Cut out the circle on the bandsaw (*see*
Fig 13.33). This blank is now ready to be
mounted on the lathe and converted into a
bangle in the method described in Chapter
8. The resulting bangle will have stripes that
follow the circumference (*see* Figs 13.34 and
13.35).

Fig 13.34   **Figs 13.34 and 13.35 A bangle with longitudinal stripes.**   Fig 13.35

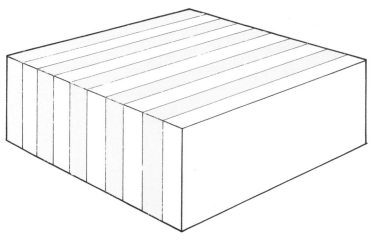

Fig 13.36 A composite block with lateral stripes. (Cut with the square face up on the bandsaw table.)

TRANSVERSE STRIPES

1 Starting with the two selected blocks of wood (again, approximately 4in [100mm]), pass each through the bandsaw sideways, i.e. with the broad face up, to produce rectangular layers of the desired width. Glue, cramp and leave to dry (*see* Figs 13.36 and 13.37).

2 When the glue is dry, cut out a circular blank as described above (*see* Figs 13.38 and 13.39). The bangle produced from such a blank will have transverse stripes (*see* Fig 13.40).

Fig 13.37 Transverse laminates glued and cramped up.

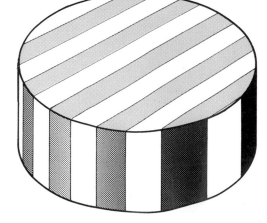

Fig 13.38   **Figs 13.38 and 13.39 A bangle blank with transverse stripes.**   **Fig 13.39**

Fig 13.40 Finished bangles with transverse stripes.

COOPERING

With this technique, wedge-shaped bands of alternating colour, rather than stripes, are produced.

1 First, decide how many segments you wish the circular blank to have. To begin with, it is probably easier to limit it to eight, until the technique has been fully mastered.

2 Select two pieces of contrasting wood and, using a bandsaw, cut each into a circular bangle blank of approximately 1in (25mm) depth and 4in (100mm) diameter.

3 Using the bandsaw, cut each blank into eight equal segments. (It is important, as with all laminating, that the sides to be glued are as flat as possible. This is especially true with coopering, so take care when bandsawing to make accurate cuts.) Taking four segments from each of the dissected blanks, fit the eight segments together in a circular fashion with the colours alternating (*see* Fig 13.41).

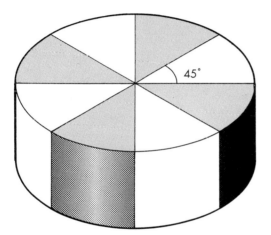

Fig 13.41 A coopered blank with eight segments.

Fig 13.42 The 'Spanish windlass' method of cramping a coopered blank.

4 Glue the segments together and cramp. There are a number of ways of cramping circular forms. It is possible to buy special cramps that have been designed for this, though it is fairly easy to improvise. Sometimes large versions of jubilee clips are used (i.e. those adjustable circular clips usually used inside cars for fastening the end of a length of rubber hose onto a rigid aperture). Alternatively, a 'Spanish windlass' can be employed. This consists of a strong piece of string or thin rope wrapped around the circumference of the blank and knotted. A small, strong stick is then passed through the string and twisted, to draw the string taut (*see* Fig 13.42). Even a number of thick, strong, elastic bands can work. The method used does not matter provided the tension is great enough to hold the segments together tightly.

5 When the glue is dry, the blank can be converted into a bangle in the usual way. The final result has bowed segments similar to those of a barrel (*see* Figs 13.44 and 13.45). *See* Note 13.4.

Laminates of unequal width can also be used very effectively with the coopering technique to produce some attractive designs (*see* Fig 13.46). In order to achieve this, the segments are cut in the usual way, then thin slices of a contrasting colour are placed in between the segments before gluing up. This will result in a small hole in the middle, but since a hole will be required there anyway, this does not matter.

Fig 13.43 A coopered bangle blank, trimmed and ready for mounting on the lathe.

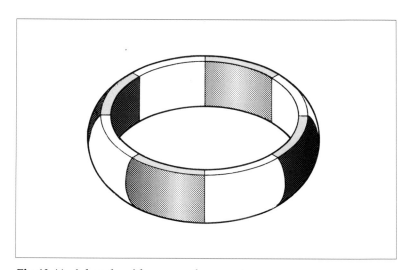

Fig 13.44 A bangle with coopered segments.

Fig 13.45 A finished coopered bangle, made from purple heart and sycamore.

NOTE 13.4 If more than eight segments are desired, then this will alter the angle at the centre of the circle. For example, ten segments would each have an angle of 36°. It is also worth considering the direction of the grain. This is not critical, and will depend upon the orientation of your segments.

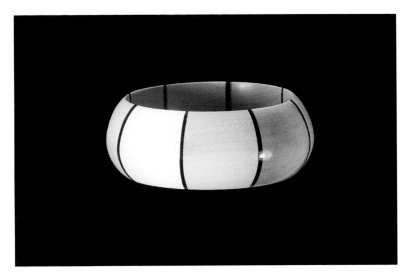

Fig 13.46 A bangle with unequal segments of sycamore and blackwood.

LAMINATING WITH SHEET METAL

Soft sheet metals can also be used as thin laminates sandwiched between layers of wood. This effect can be extremely attractive, especially if the colour of the metal contrasts well with the colour of the wood. For example, silver or pewter looks beautiful with ebony (*see* Figs 13.47 and 13.48).

Ordinary superglue, or epoxy resin, will be sufficient to bond the metal to wood in the usual way, and some metal laminates turn almost as easily as the wood, though they do have a tendency to blunt the tools, so frequent tool sharpening is advisable. The width of the sheet metal is not crucial, but approximately ⅟₃₂in (1mm) works very well.

Fig 13.47 Earrings with pewter laminates set diagonally.

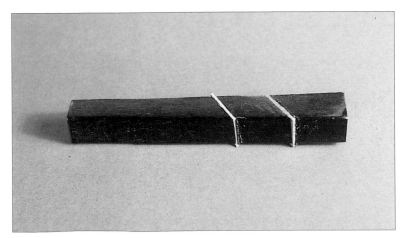

Fig 13.48 Layers of pewter glued diagonally into an ebony piano key.

Pewter is a soft metal and turns easily. Copper, being harder, is a little more difficult to turn. Brass is harder still. Brass, in fact, can be quite difficult to turn, especially as a laminate, because it offers much greater resistance to the tool blade compared to wood. To make things easier, before mounting the laminated blank on the lathe, file off all the protruding metal edges with a small metal file.

Fig 13.49 An earring with diagonal laminates of copper and brass.

SOME FINAL THOUGHTS ON LAMINATING

With further experimentation, other laminated designs can be produced. However, remember that complicated patterns do not necessarily produce the best effects when converted into jewellery. It is best to keep things simple when working on a small scale. You will also find that the patterns can look very different when a square-section, laminated blank is turned into a cylinder on the lathe, so it is worth trying a few simple patterns first.

The composite blanks can be used in a variety of ways to produce different designs of jewellery, as can be seen from the photographs. Some very attractive geometric designs can be created by using the bandsaw to cut the blanks into thinner pieces of the desired shape; for example, triangles (*see* Fig 13.50).

TAKE CARE

If blanks are to be turned on the lathe it is *very important* to take extreme care during the turning process, especially when turning between centres. This is because, even with very strong glue, each blank has, in effect, layers of potential weak spots along its length. Excessive strain put on the blank during turning can result in breaks occurring, especially with items such as long earrings.

In order to avoid this, ensure that all gaps are filled with a strong, gap-filling glue. A viscous superglue is ideal, but any strong thick glue will work. You may need to check the blank at intervals during roughing down to see if any new gaps have appeared. Also, make sure that your tools are extremely sharp, and only remove small amounts of wood, with light, even strokes, avoiding any pressure on the blank. It is more difficult to produce long, thin-stemmed items with laminated wood, due to these weaknesses. So if you are making long earrings, it is wise to keep the stems at a reasonable thickness. If you should find that the blank does break, all is not lost. It can be repaired with superglue and re-mounted on the lathe later. Patience and perseverance will eventually pay off.

Sometimes the laminates will shift slightly during the first few days after completion. This tends to happen if you have used a PVA-type glue (Cascamite does not tend to do this). It will not alter the appearance but it will affect the *feel* of the object since slight ridges will have formed. If this has happened, you may wish to re-sand the item to remove the ridges and then reapply the finish. Alternatively, after turning, leave the final sanding for a few days until any shifting has taken place, then do the final sanding and finishing. It is by no means necessary to do either of these things, since the appearance of the object is unaffected, and the ridges are only very slight. However, one of the most appealing features of wood is its tactile qualities, and in view of this, many people would want to ensure a perfectly smooth finish.

Fig 13.50 Geometric designs made from laminate slices cut out on the bandsaw.

14
Other Decorative Techniques

- Beading
- Scorch rings
- Inlaying wood banding
- Upholstery nails
- Glass beads, marbles and gemstones
- Spray paint
- Metallic ink, paints, pastes and powders
- Gold leaf
- Thin wire
- Carving on turning

LEVEL OF SKILL: Intermediate

THIS CHAPTER DESCRIBES a variety of different techniques that can be used to decorate items of jewellery. Decisions about whether to use any of these techniques will depend upon the type of wood that has been used, and the overall design of the object. In some cases, further decoration would be inappropriate. For example, if the wood has a highly attractive grain pattern, or if the object is extremely small, then any further decoration would appear clumsy. Sometimes, an object is best left plain in order for the form to be fully appreciated.

Having said that, there are many occasions when further decoration can enhance the overall appearance and make the item generally more interesting. This is particularly true when plain timbers have been used, and additional detail can add to the appeal.

There are many techniques for further decoration, and it is very important that the technique chosen is appropriate for the item concerned. The following list of techniques is by no means an exhaustive one. There is no limit to the number of things that can be tried; again, it is all down to experimentation. I have attempted to select those procedures that I have found most effective, easy, and applicable.

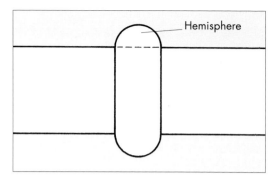

Fig 14.1 The bead should form a neat hemisphere.

BEADING

By 'beading' I mean the procedure of turning a 'bead' on the surface of the wood by means of a skew chisel or a beading tool. (A sharp parting tool can also be used.) I do not intend to give details of how to turn beads here, since I am assuming that readers will already have that skill, or can acquire it elsewhere.

For the best visual effect, beads should be fully rounded and should ideally form a hemisphere in cross section (*see* Fig 14.1). A single bead can be very effective, or perhaps a series of beads gradually increasing or decreasing in size. (*See* Figs 5.13–5.14 on page 31 for examples of 'balanced' and 'unbalanced' beading.)

Fig 14.2 Various items (made from wenge, rosewood and purple heart) where beading has been used as a form of decoration.

If you are creating beads that gradually decrease in size, be very careful to bear in mind the overall width of the wood at the point of the thinnest bead. If the wood is quite thin at this point (for example at the outer edge of a bangle or at the tip of a pointed earring or brooch), there is the distinct possibility that a very fine bead will break off unless the wood is very strong. Bear in mind, also, the type of wood that is being used. A soft, coarse-grained wood is less suitable for fine beading than a dense, fine-grained one.

SCORCH RINGS

The use of scorch rings can be quite effective on plain, light-coloured timbers such as maple or lime. The technique is extremely simple:

1 With the lathe running, and using the point of a parting tool or similar, make a thin groove in the surface of the wood (*see* Fig 14.3).

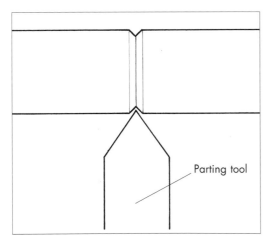

Fig 14.3 Make a thin groove in the surface of the wood, using a parting tool.

2 Take a piece of thin steel wire and, with the lathe still running, place this in the groove and hold it there under pressure. Do not let your fingers come in contact with the wood. The wire should be held between the fingers on either side of the wood (*see* Figs 14.4 and 14.5).

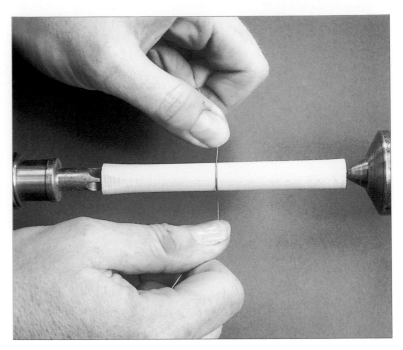

Fig 14.4 Making a scorch ring.

3 After a few seconds the wood will start to scorch where the wire has created friction heat in the groove. The wire may now be removed, to reveal a brown-black scorch ring in the groove. If the ring is uneven in appearance, repeat the procedure for a further few seconds until the scorching effect is even. Do not let the wood become over-scorched, since it will tend to darken on either side of the line and this will spoil the effect.

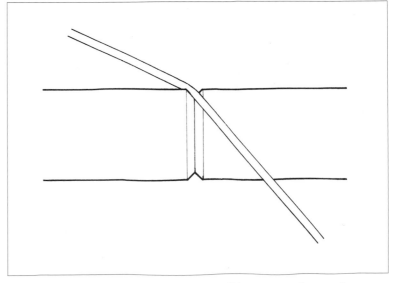

Fig 14.5 Hold the wire in the groove until it scorches the wood.

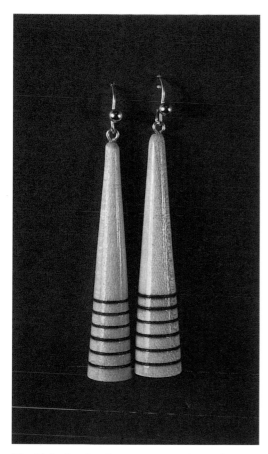

Fig 14.6 **A pair of sycamore earrings where scorch rings have been used to decorate the otherwise plain surface.**

INLAYING WOOD BANDING

There is quite a variety of different wood bandings available commercially, which have been produced specifically for woodworkers. These bandings can be obtained either as a single plain line (in various widths) or as composite bandings where two or more different-coloured timbers have been assembled to form an attractive patterned strip. The width of the bandings can vary from about ⅟32in (1mm) for a plain strip to ⅜in (10mm) for the wider and more complicated designs, and the prices vary accordingly. These bandings are not suitable for objects with a small diameter because the banding will snap if bent too sharply. But for more gentle curves, such as around the circumference of a bangle, they are ideal.

See Note 14.1.

The procedure for inlaying wood bandings is as follows:

1 With the lathe running, and using a parting tool, make a shallow groove in the surface of the wood. This groove should be exactly the same width and depth as the banding.

2 Using cyanoacrylate glue, glue one end of the banding in place in the groove. Hold this firmly until the glue has set (*see* Fig 14.7).

NOTE 14.1 By soaking the wood banding, pre-bending it, then letting it dry prior to use, snapping can be avoided, because the banding has been made flexible enough to be bent round smaller diameters, although not *very* small diameters.

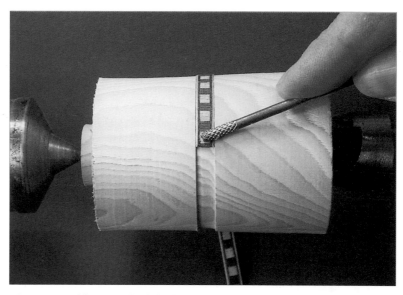

Fig 14.7 **Hold one end of the banding in place until the glue has set.**

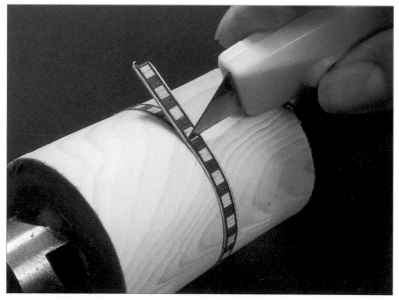

Fig 14.8 **Cut the free end at the exact point of overlap.**

Fig 14.9 Sycamore bangles with inlaid wood banding.

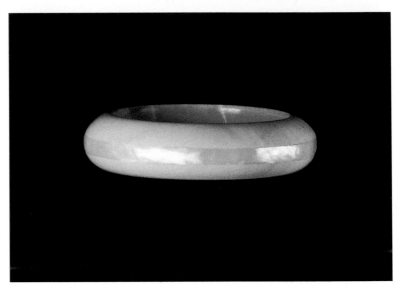

Fig 14.10 A sycamore bangle with inlaid 'mother–of–pearl–effect' banding.

Fig 14.11 A bangle decorated with upholstery nails.

3 Apply glue to the rest of the groove and gradually press the remainder of the banding in place. There will be a short length overlapping, which can be cut off when the rest of the banding has set in place and the glue has dried.

4 Using a sharp blade, cut the excess banding at the point where it meets the first end, so that the two ends meet exactly (*see* Fig 14.8).

5 Glue the loose end firmly in place.

As an alternative to wood, it is possible to buy banding made of simulated mother-of-pearl. This can be used in exactly the same way as wood banding (*see* Fig 14.10).

UPHOLSTERY NAILS

Upholstery nails are the round-headed brass nails often used in antique furniture, particularly chairs, to fasten the fabric to the wooden frame. These can easily be used to add decoration to jewellery. The shafts tend to be rather long so it is a good idea to saw them down to a more suitable length. Mark the place where each nail is to be inserted, drill a small pilot hole of the same diameter as the shaft of the nail, and glue the nail shaft into the hole. A couple of light taps with a hammer will help to seat the nail properly.

GLASS BEADS, MARBLES AND GEMSTONES

Glass beads, small marbles and gemstones can all be used to decorate wooden jewellery. This is a straightforward procedure. The diameter of the bead, marble, or stone is measured, and an appropriate-sized hole is drilled in the turned item. The bead, marble, or stone is then inserted into the hole and glued into place. Although this procedure is straightforward, there are one or two details that need to be considered.

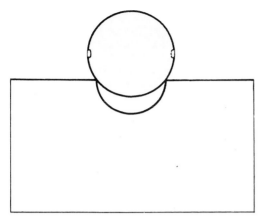

Fig 14.12 If the drilled hole is too small, the bead will be seated too high and the holes in the bead will be visible.

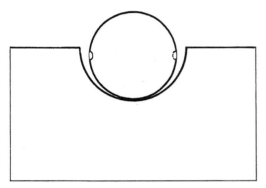

Fig 14.13 If the drilled hole is too large, the bead will be seated too deeply and there will be gaps around the sides.

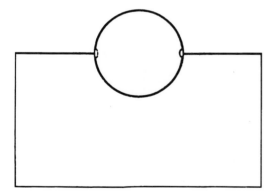

Fig 14.14 The correctly seated bead.

SPHERICAL BEADS

Most of the beads that I use for decoration are made of glass, though I often use haematite beads because these can look particularly attractive. The only problem with using beads is the fact that they have a hole drilled through. In order to disguise this it is necessary to take great care with the inlaying procedure:

Measure the diameter of the bead and drill a hole of the same size in the item of jewellery at the point where the bead is to be embedded. The size and depth of the hole are critical. It must be the *exact* diameter of the bead and the depth must be equal to exactly half the width of the bead. If the hole is too small, the bead will be seated too high and the threading holes on the sides of the bead will be apparent (*see* Fig 14.12). If the hole is too big, the bead will be seated too low and there will be a gap around the edge (*see* Fig 14.13). If the hole is exactly the right size, the bead will sit neatly in place, and if the holes are aligned horizontally they will be almost flush with the surface of the wood and therefore barely visible (*see* Fig 14.14). The beads can then be glued into place with cyanoacrylate glue.

GEMSTONES

Polished semiprecious stones can come in a variety of shapes. Because they are to be inserted into a pre-drilled hole you will need to use those that have been cut into a hemisphere; in other words, where the cross section is circular and not oval. Suppliers of cut and polished stones can be hard to find, but some jewellers who make their own jewellery (especially silver as opposed to gold) sometimes sell them or can order them. Some craft shops also sell them.

Fig 14.15 Ebony earrings and ring with inlaid haematite beads.

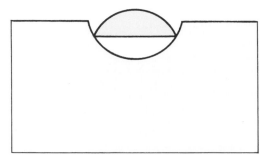

Fig 14.16 If the drilled hole is too deep, the stone will be seated too low and there will be gaps around the sides.

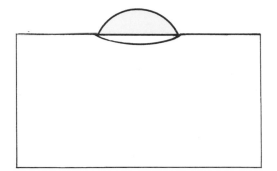

Fig 14.17 The correctly seated stone.

Only a very shallow hole will need to be drilled into the wood. If the hole is drilled too deep, the stone will be seated too low and there will be a gap surrounding the stone (*see* Fig 14.16). The diameter of the hole should be exactly the same size as the diameter of the base of the stone (*see* Fig 14.17). The stones are glued in place in the same way as beads.

MARBLES

Most marbles will be too large for jewellery but it is possible to find relatively small ones, often with an attractive metallic surface, and these can be used quite effectively on larger items. The holes are drilled in the same way as for beads, except that there are, of course, no holes in the marbles that need to be aligned horizontally.

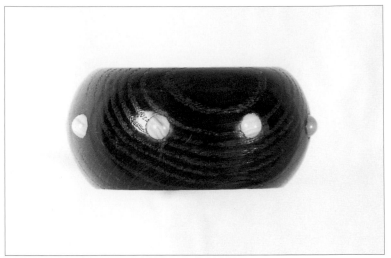

Fig 14.18 A stained-oak bangle inlaid with blue lace agate gemstones.

Fig 14.19 An ebony ring inlaid with a turquoise stone.

Fig 14.20 A purple-heart brooch inlaid with a quartz stone.

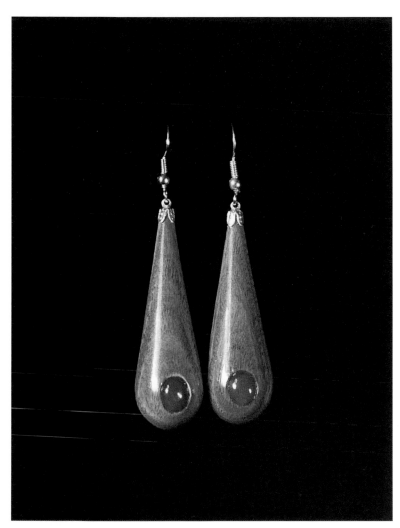

Fig 14.21 A pair of lignum-vitae earrings inlaid with jade stones. Jade was deliberately chosen to enhance the greenish colour of the wood. Note that the stones are oval, not round. As a result, the holes in this example had to be cut by hand in order to receive the stones.

Fig 14.22 An acacia bangle decorated with black spray paint.

SPRAY PAINT

In most circumstances I would steer clear of spray paint, for the reasons outlined in Chapter 11. However, there are exceptions to every rule, and this is one. Black spray paint with a satin finish, of the type produced for cars, can give an attractive appearance to woodturned items in general, including jewellery. This effect is, of course, a matter of personal taste and will possibly not appeal to the purists. When spraying, ensure that the can is held at a reasonable distance from the object and keep the spray can moving. Do not over-spray since this will cause drips. Do a small area at a time, leave to dry, then spray the next area. It is a good idea to place the object to be sprayed inside a large cardboard box that has been placed on its side. This helps to contain the spray and minimizes the mess. Fig 14.22 shows a bangle that has been sprayed in the manner described.

A beautiful metallic effect can be created if iron paste (of the type used for polishing cast iron fireplaces) is rubbed into the surface of an object that has previously been sprayed with black paint. By buffing with a soft cloth, an attractive sheen will be produced. Items decorated in this way will need to be sprayed with melamine spray afterwards because the iron paste tends to rub off unless a sealing finish is applied.

METALLIC INKS, PAINTS, PASTES AND POWDERS

Gold and silver marker pens with extra fine points are very useful for decorating jewellery. Patterns can be drawn or stencilled onto the surface of the wood. Lines, dots and circles can be added to enhance the shape of the piece, with the help of masking tape, if very straight lines are required. These are very simple decorative techniques which can look extremely effective (*see* Figs 14.24 and 14.25).

Fig 14.23 A sycamore bangle illustrating the 'metallic' effect.

Fig 14.24 Two pairs of earrings and a brooch, decorated with gold and silver marker pens. The wood is holly which has been dyed with Indian ink.

Metallic paints and powders can also be tried in a variety of ways to produce similar effects. Metallic paints can be used to good effect when applied sparingly, to enhance or highlight a small portion of the item, such as a rim, a bead, the edges of a groove, etc.

Metallic pastes and powders can be rubbed into grooves and also into the grain of wood to produce interesting effects. If powder is to be used, a thin layer of cyanoacrylate glue applied to the crevice first will help the powder to adhere.

Metallic products should be used sparingly to produce the best aesthetic results, otherwise the effect can be rather overdone.

GOLD LEAF

Gold leaf is extremely difficult to apply and a great deal of practice and patience is required to produce a successful result. The process of gilding dates back many centuries and the technique used to require a long apprenticeship before it could be said to be fully mastered. Gold leaf is extremely fine

Fig 14.25 Two beads that have been decorated by rubbing their surfaces with gold paste. (Melamine should be applied to the surface to prevent the paste from rubbing off.)

and is therefore very difficult to cut and to handle. It is applied delicately to a surface that has previously been coated with special 'size' to which the leaf adheres. With patience the application of gold leaf can produce stunning effects, but I would recommend that the reader refers to a book on the subject before embarking upon the procedure (*see* bibliography on page 147).

THIN WIRE

With imagination, very thin wire can be used to good effect in a variety of ways. For example, it can be carefully wound around an item as a form of decoration (*see* Fig 14.27).

CARVING ON TURNING

For those who have the skill, many items of jewellery can be carved as a means of decorating the surface. Fig 14.28 shows a bangle that has been roughly carved and then sprayed. This particular style of carving is called 'chip carving' and involves removing small triangles of wood using a sharp blade. A Stanley knife was the only tool used in this example.

This chapter has described a few ideas for decorating turned jewellery. However, this is by no means a complete list. There is really no limit to the variety of different techniques that can be tried. All that is required is imagination and a willingness to experiment.

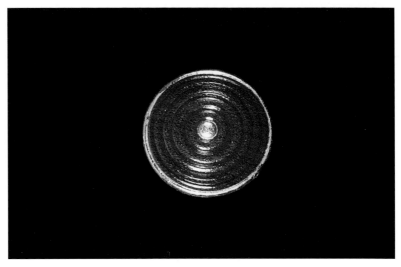

Fig 14.26 A purple-heart brooch decorated with gold leaf.

Fig 14.27 An ebony earring decorated with thin copper wire.

Fig 14.28 A bangle decorated with carving.

15
Finishing Techniques

- Sanding
- Applying a finish
- A final polish

I T IS PARTICULARLY important to achieve a good finish on small items such as jewellery, because they are often examined closely and, because of their size, any defects tend to show up very easily.

Most turners seem to have their own preferred methods of finishing which they find work well for them, and it is not my intention here to go into much detail on finishing techniques. With jewellery, however, there are one or two special considerations that need to be taken into account. This chapter has been subdivided into two sections; the first deals with sanding, and the second concentrates on applying finishes.

SANDING

The basic principles of sanding that apply to other forms of turning also apply to small items such as jewellery. There are not the same difficulties as one might experience with the insides of bowls; indeed, sanding is a straightforward matter provided one remembers to avoid the pitfalls. Always keep the abrasive paper moving over the surface, and try to sand with a light touch, in order to avoid scratch marks. It is also important to use the finest grade of abrasive that will do the job.

GRADES OF ABRASIVE GRIT
Which grade of grit you choose will depend upon a number of factors, such as the type of wood, the tool that has been used, and the quality of the surface finish straight from the tool (which in turn depends on the degree of skill of the turner). On items of jewellery I rarely use a grit coarser than 180 and I usually start off with around 240 or less, then work through the grades up to about 400, finishing off with a very fine grade of wire wool, usually 00000. On materials other than wood, such as cow horn, bone, acrylic, metal, corion, etc., I finish up with 1000 grit wet-and-dry paper (used wet), followed by a polish with ordinary metal polish.

OVERSANDING
Oversanding is a common fault. Some woods can tolerate a great deal of sanding, while

others cannot. Purple heart and yew, in particular, will readily produce heat cracks when the wood begins to get too hot. Once the wood has cracked, there is very little that can be done about it. Thin superglue trickled into the crack will hold it together but it rarely disguises it. (Remember also to coat the surrounding surface area with your finishing liquid before applying superglue, otherwise the wood will stain.)

It is far better to prevent the cracks from occurring in the first place, either by having a little more patience and giving the wood a chance to cool off or, better still, by trying to improve one's turning skills so that less sanding is required! However, these things are easier said than done, and we all make mistakes from time to time.

ABRASIVE PAPERS
There are many different types of abrasive paper available, and most turners have their own preferences. I tend to use cloth-backed abrasive, which I find works well for me. I would recommend trying various types and comparing the effects of each in different circumstances.

SAFETY
Finally, it is of course essential to have adequate protection against the inhalation of dust. If a proper dust extraction system is not feasible, then at least try to minimize the amount of dust being inhaled by the use of alternative safety devices such as respiratory helmets, masks, etc. This is particularly important when turning tropical timbers, metals, animal products such as bone and horn, and man-made substances such as acrylic and corion. *See* Chapter 1 for a discussion of safety devices.

APPLYING A FINISH

Before deciding which type of finish to use, there are a number of factors that need to be considered:

THE DESIRED FINAL APPEARANCE
Do you want the item to have a glossy or a satin finish? This is a matter of personal

preference, although there are good reasons for choosing a highly polished look for jewellery. One is that the colours are enhanced by a shinier surface, and another is that, traditionally, jewellery has always tended to be made from highly polished materials, such as metals and precious stones. We associate jewellery with things that shine and sparkle. Small items are sometimes overlooked if they have insufficient shine. So although I might tend to select a duller, satin finish for a bowl, perhaps, I would always choose a more highly polished effect for jewellery.

DURABILITY

Unlike some turned objects, which are created purely as an art form, jewellery is designed to be worn. Favourite pieces of jewellery are worn often. Consequently they are subjected to a certain amount of wear and tear, and a lot of handling. This is worth bearing in mind when selecting a finish. Sanding sealer followed by a coat of wax (preferably carnauba wax – beeswax is less durable) is fine, though I tend to use melamine instead of sanding sealer as it produces an excellent finish, is very durable, and waterproof. For the same reasons I sometimes use Rustin's plastic coating.

WATER RESISTANCE

Any finish applied to jewellery should ideally be waterproof. This is especially true for bangles which frequently get wet if they are worn while doing the washing-up, for example! (Personally, I would recommend that bangles are *removed* before washing up, but we can all be forgetful at times.)

Of all the various types of jewellery, bangles are the most likely to get knocked about. For that reason they really need an exceptionally tough finish. I always use Rustin's plastic coating on bangles, since it gives a high degree of protection and is totally waterproof. It is also a versatile finish, because you can control the degree of gloss. I usually use two or three coats, rubbed down after each coat with fine wire wool, and polished up afterwards with the abrasive liquid. This gives an attractive sheen. The

final rub down with wire wool is very important, not only to produce a good, smooth surface, but also to prevent the item from looking 'varnished'. A surface which is *too* glossy looks cheap. Plastic coating, although a little time consuming to apply, does create a nice-looking finish which is more durable than any other.

THE USE OF STAINS, DYES, PAINTS AND INKS

Wood that has been treated with dye or stain cannot necessarily be given the type of finish that you would normally use on unstained wood. An oil-based finish, for example, cannot be used on top of an oil-based dye. The same is true of spirit-based dyes and finishes. This is because the finish will dissolve the dye underneath if both substances have the same base (*see* Chapter 11).

Similarly, if you have used certain paints, powders or inks, it is likely that these will be removed by the application of finishes such as sanding sealer or melamine. It it wise, therefore, to test out the effects beforehand on a piece of scrap wood. Melamine spray is very useful as a finish for wood that has been decorated with inks, paints or dyes. Even though ordinary melamine applied with a cloth might remove the colour, by partially dissolving it and wiping it away, used as a spray it sits on top without disturbing the decoration beneath. It is important not to touch the surface until the spray is thoroughly dry but, after that, another coat will seal it in effectively.

A FINAL POLISH

For the types of finish described above, a further polish is not really necessary. However, from time to time, some objects will need to be given a bit of a polish to keep them looking at their best, particularly if they have seen some wear and tear. A beeswax-based polish is good for this and there are many to choose from. Avoid cellulose-based products (which usually come in the form of aerosols) because these can have an adverse effect on some finishes.

CHAPTER

16
Jewellery Findings

- Earring wires
- Eyelets
- Earposts and scrolls
- Earring clasps
- Ear screws

- Ear clips
- Brooch backs
- Lapel pins
- Jump rings
- Necklace clasps

EWELLERY FINDINGS are the metal attachments fitted on items of jewellery that enable them to be attached to the wearer. They include brooch pins or backs, earring wires, earposts, stick pins, clasps, fasteners and eyelet rings.

Before purchasing your jewellery findings, it is worth considering the type of metal you wish them to be made from. With items such as brooch backs, it is not really important, since they do not show and do not come into contact with the skin. But with earring wires and earposts, which are most commonly available in pure silver, silver plated, or base metal, a little more thought needs to be given. Because the wire comes into contact with the skin, it is often wise to purchase pure silver, or at least silver plate, as opposed to base metal. This is because some people have allergic reactions to base metal and if this is worn in the ears for any length of time it can cause irritation and redness. It would be a great pity to have laboured long and hard over a pair of earrings for someone, only to discover that they could not wear them! Not everyone is allergic to base metal, however, and many people find that they can wear any metal, provided that it is not for too long. So perhaps it is worth finding out beforehand, provided the recipient is known to you. If the item is to be put up for sale it is best to play safe and avoid base metal.

Another consideration is the colour of the metal. If you have inlaid the item of jewellery with wire of some description, it is better to choose jewellery findings of the same colour to match. Also, some woods look better with silver-coloured metals, while others are enhanced more by a gold colour.

Jewellery findings can be obtained from craft shops that stock jewellery-making equipment (e.g. beads and so forth), but they can also be obtained through mail order. A brief description of various types of jewellery finding follows:

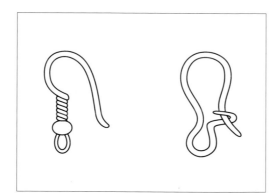

Fig 16.1

Fig 16.3

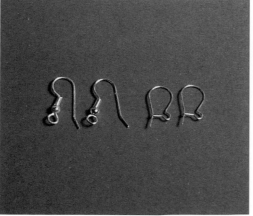

Figs 16.1 and 16.2 Ear wires.   **Fig 16.2**

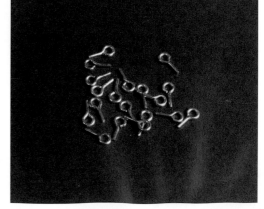

Figs 16.3 and 16.4 Eyelets.   **Fig 16.4**

Fig 16.5

Figs 16.5 and 16.6 Earposts and scrolls. **Fig 16.6**

EARRING WIRES (OR EAR WIRES)

These are the hooped wires that fit through the holes in the earlobe, from which pendant-type earrings are suspended. They usually have a small loop which is threaded through an eyelet in the top of the earring.

EYELETS

These are small hoops on a short stalk that are inserted into the top of the earring to provide an attachment for the earring wires. Again, they are mainly used for the pendant style of earring.

EARPOSTS AND SCROLLS

These are used for the stud type of earring. The earpost is a thin, short stick of wire attached to a flat plate. The plate is attached to the centre back of the earring and the stick is inserted through the hole in the earlobe. The scroll is a device that is pushed tightly onto the stick on the other side of the earlobe and ensures that the earring is secure.

EARRING CLASPS

These are used in conjunction with pendant earrings and serve the same function as the eyelets, providing an attachment for the earring wires. However, they are rather more ornamental and consist of four decorative 'fingers' which can be compressed to literally 'clasp' the top of the earring. They need to be glued in place.

EAR SCREWS

These are attachments for the benefit of those people who do not have pierced ears. A wire loop has an eyelet or clasp which is attached to the top of the earring. The other end of the loop has a screw device which screws into the back of the earlobe to secure it in place. (Rather uncomfortable!)

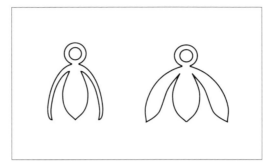

Fig 16.7

Figs 16.7 and 16.8 Earring clasps. **Fig 16.8**

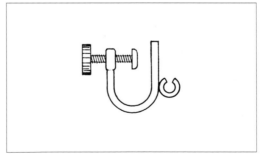

Fig 16.9

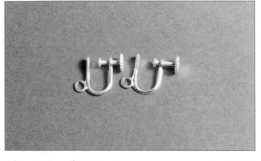

Figs 16.9 and 16.10 Ear screws. **Fig 16.10**

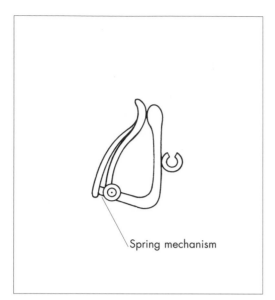

Fig 16.11

Figs 16.11 and 16.12 Ear clips.   **Fig 16.12**

EAR CLIPS

Also for the benefit of those without pierced ears, these are a (slightly) more comfortable alternative to earscrews. They have a flat plate or clasp at one end of the hoop and a spring clip at the other. The pressure of the spring clip keeps the earring secure.

BROOCH BACKS

These come in various designs but their function is the same. They are glued to the centre back of a brooch and consist of a sprung pin and clasp, enabling the brooch to be attached to the wearer's clothing.

LAPEL PINS

These are an alternative to the brooch back and are most suitable for those items that are too small to be used in conjunction with a conventional brooch back. They consist of a stout pin which is attached to a flat plate, on to which is glued the wooden item. The stick is inserted into the clothing and a cylindrical 'protector' is pushed snugly onto the pointed end to secure the whole in place. Sometimes it is not convenient to have a flat plate on the end. An alternative is to saw off the plate and insert the head of the stick pin directly into a hole that has been drilled into the bottom of the wooden item. A cheaper alternative is to use an ordinary large needle in conjunction with a protector (*see* Fig 16.16).

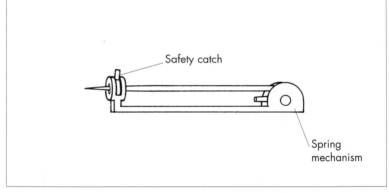

Fig 16.13

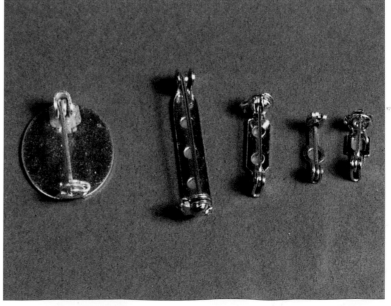

Figs 16.13 and 16.14 Brooch backs.   **Fig 16.14**

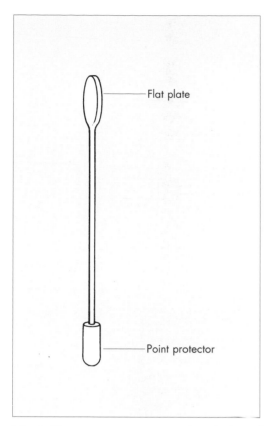

Fig 16.15

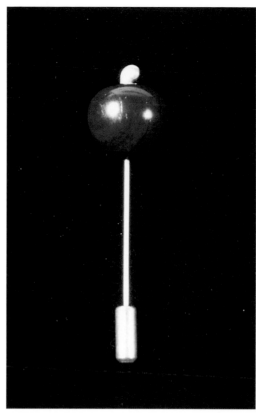

Figs 16.15 and 16.16 Lapel pin.

Fig 16.16

JUMP RINGS

These are small metal rings that can be used in conjunction with any of the above, wherever appropriate.

NECKLACE CLASPS

These take a variety of forms, the most common of which is shown in Fig 16.17.

The above articles are those most commonly available from suppliers, but this is by no means an exhaustive list. There are many variations on these basic themes as well as other items, such as various designs of fastenings for necklaces, for example. Before purchasing any of the above, it is often useful to browse through a catalogue, if possible, to see just what is available. Catalogues containing jewellery findings are available from various suppliers.

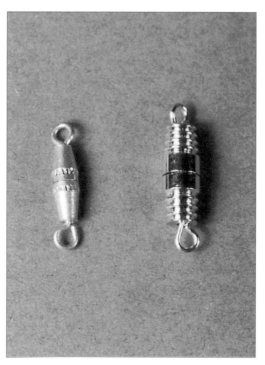

Fig 16.17 Necklace clasps.

17
Turning Alternative Materials

- ▌ Bone
- ▌ Cow horn
- ▌ Tagua nut
- ▌ Metal
- ▌ Acrylic
- ▌ Corion
- ▌ Composite coloured laminates

ALTHOUGH THE PRIMARY focus of this book is on turning jewellery from wood, it is often interesting to experiment with other materials. Some very attractive results can be gained by turning jewellery from other substances and it can be fun learning how different materials respond to being turned. This chapter explores a number of different materials that can be successfully turned to create interesting and unusual jewellery.

When turning any of the following materials, it is absolutely essential to take full precautions against the inhalation of dust.

BONE

Bone has been used in turning for hundreds of years. Examples typically include small decorative objects such as buttons, needlecases, knobs, handles, lace bobbins, crotchet hooks, knitting needles, and various ornaments. It is only possible to produce fairly small items because bones, even from larger animals, tend to be of insufficient

Fig 17.1 Bone earrings with silver-wire inlay.

width to produce anything of substantial size. In addition, the leg bones of animals are hollow, so any solid piece must come from the side of the shank.

SOURCES

One source of bone is, of course, a butcher. The thigh bones of larger animals such as bullock, are suitable, but it is often a case of taking whatever is available. The preparation is rather tedious. The bone must be boiled to remove the flesh, and then bleached. To bleach bone, leave it soaking in hydrogen peroxide (available from chemists) for several days. This removes the oil from the bone. A bandsaw is then required to saw it up into suitable-sized blanks. Not all bone derived from this source is suitable, however. It is common to encounter bone that is too porous and full of tiny holes. Inevitably, there is much wastage, but since old bones from the butcher are usually fairly cheap, the wastage is more in terms of time than money.

However, if messing around with old bones from the butcher does not appeal, there is another source: suppliers of lace bobbin blanks sometimes stock bone blanks. These are often made from reconstituted bone, but they turn reasonably well. The drawback with lace bobbin blanks is that they are very narrow. Nevertheless, they are ideal for long earrings (*see* Fig 17.1).

PREPARATION AND TURNING

Bone is extremely hard and brittle, so in order to render it easier to turn, it is necessary to boil it for an hour or so prior to turning. You can leave it to soak for a few days if it is not to be turned immediately, but if left soaking for too long it will become discoloured. Even after boiling and soaking, bone is still much harder and more brittle than wood, so great care must be taken during the roughing down stage. Apart from that, the turning procedure is the same as for wood. Once the blank has been roughed down to a cylinder it becomes remarkably

NOTE 17.1 If you are intending to leave an almost finished item attached to the rest of the blank by a thin spigot (for example, while sanding and finishing), it is worth noting that a thicker spigot is required for cow horn than is normally required for wood. If the cow horn spigot is too fine, it will break off since it does not possess the strength of wood fibres.

easy to turn. Sometimes the bone is discoloured deeper within the blank, and darker patches can occur as turning continues. However, these can be bleached out afterwards. The surface quality of the finished item is difficult to predict and can vary considerably from one piece to the next. Sometimes you can end up with a beautifully smooth, unblemished piece. At other times, a close examination of the surface will reveal that it is pitted.

FINISHING AND DECORATION

After the item has been turned, it can be sanded in the same way as wood, but it may need to be bleached again to remove any small, discoloured patches. Soak it in hydrogen peroxide for an hour or two if necessary. I then finish it off by scrubbing it with toothpaste and giving it a final polish with metal polish. This last procedure may sound a little surprising but it really does produce a beautiful finish. However, take care to use clean cloths, otherwise you run the risk of discolouring the bone all over again.

Bone can be decorated in the same way as wood. It can be stained, beaded, scorched, inlaid with wire, etc. (*see* Chapter 14). If you

inlay wire, you must be careful not to leave the finished item in bleach for too long, since the bleach will eventually dissolve the metal. It can also affect the glue sometimes, causing the wire to become loosened from its bed.

COW HORN

Horn can be difficult to obtain, although some specialist timber merchants who sell turning supplies do sell it. Since horns are hollow, except at the tips, the same problems of size are encountered as with bone. In other words, only small items can be turned. If a solid object is required, the tips of the horns will yield the largest solid mass. These can be sawn off with a bandsaw and glued to a wooden faceplate (*see* page 24 and Figs 17.2 and 17.3).

Horn is quite soft, and is easy to turn, though it has a rather unpleasant odour. It takes an excellent polish and some very attractive pieces of jewellery can be made from it. It comes in a variety of colours, ranging from charcoal black with lighter flecks, through shades of grey to a beautiful amber which resembles tortoiseshell. It is turned in exactly the same way as wood, though during the finishing stage I usually end with an exceptionally fine grade of abrasive (1000 grit wet-and-dry) and a final polish using ordinary metal polish on a cloth. It will buff up to a mirror finish.

See Note 17.1.

Cow horn

Wooden faceplate screwed to metal faceplate

Fig 17.2   **Figs 17.2 and 17.3 A piece of horn mounted on a wooden faceplate.**   **Fig 17.3**

TAGUA NUT

This is also known as 'vegetable ivory' or 'palm nut'. Tagua nuts (which originate from South America and parts of Africa) are sometimes sold in bags by specialist timber merchants who sell turning supplies. Each nut is oval in shape and about 2in (50mm) long by 1in (25mm) thick. On the outside of each nut is a thin brown skin, but inside it is pure white.

Tagua nuts are extremely hard and dense, but surprisingly soft to turn. In fact, they are a sheer delight to turn, and produce wonderful long, white shavings. They take a good polish and a high gloss can easily be obtained. 'Vegetable ivory' is quite an apt description since they have the appearance of ivory, if perhaps a little whiter.

They have been used for a long time in the button industry, especially in France, Austria, England and America. Ornamental turners have also used tagua nuts for decorative items such as thimbles and miniatures of all descriptions.

Like bone and horn, the size of object that can be turned from a tagua nut is fairly limited, and an additional drawback is that they have a hollow area in the centre. This can vary in size from quite large to hardly noticeable. Unfortunately, it is not possible to detect the size of the hollow area from the outside. However, if one end is sawn off, one can get an indication. The end of each nut is, in any case, usually sawn off prior to turning, otherwise their irregular shape makes them impossible to chuck (unless you wish to turn them between centres). The flat end produced by the saw is either glued to a piece of wood which is then mounted in the chuck, or glued directly to a wooden faceplate (in the same fashion as for horn, described above).

The size, shape, and hollowness of tagua nuts limit the size and shape of the item that can be turned and, with the ones with large areas of hollow, there can often be some wastage. However, they are quite suitable for

Fig 17.4 Various items turned from horn.

rings and brooches (*see* Fig 17.5 and 17.6). You may find that the brooches have a slightly irregular hollow area on the back caused by the fissure inside the nut. This can easily be filled with superglue and sanded flat. Because of the colour of tagua nut and the high gloss that can be achieved, it really can yield some extremely attractive items and, although they can be a little difficult to turn, for the reasons mentioned, it is worth persevering.

Fig 17.5 A tagua nut glued to scrap wood and supported in a four-jaw contracting chuck.

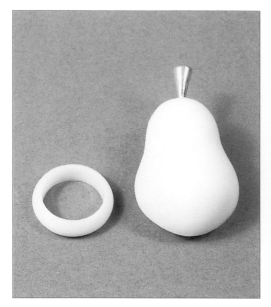

Fig 17.6 A tagua-nut ring and brooch.

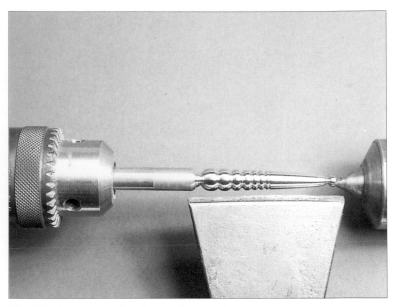

Fig 17.7 Turning a ring from a brass rod.

METAL

Metal can be satisfactorily turned on an ordinary wood lathe provided that the metal is a soft one. (Steel, for example, would be no good because it is too hard.) Soft metals can be quite easy to turn but they do tend to blunt the tools rather more readily than wood does, so it is necessary to sharpen them more frequently than usual. Brass can be turned successfully but, because it is not particularly soft, it is very slow (*see* Figs 17.7 and 17.8). Pewter on the other hand, because it is extremely soft, turns beautifully. In fact, it is a delight to turn, producing wonderfully fine, long shavings. Pewter will polish up well and resembles silver, with the advantage that it does not tarnish (*see* Fig 17.9). Copper is harder than pewter but softer than brass.

When turning is complete, the metals can be sanded in the same way as wood, but finish up with a high-speed polish with any ordinary metal polish. Remember that metal is much heavier than wood, so do not be tempted to make items that are too large, or they will be too heavy and cumbersome to wear. This is particularly true with earrings (unless it is your desire to have elongated earlobes!).

It can be difficult to obtain suitable metals for turning. Brass stair rod can sometimes be found, and Yellow Pages will often list dealers in non-ferrous metals who occasionally have offcuts. Other than that, one can always resort to the usual standby of car-boot sales, jumble sales, and other similar events, which can occasionally present one with useful treasures.

See Note 17.2.

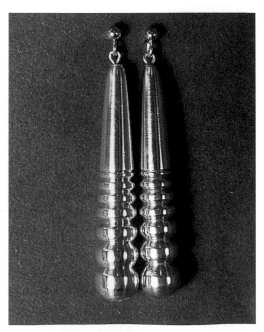

Fig 17.8 Brass earrings.

NOTE 17.2 Special care should be taken when turning metal. Make absolutely sure that the blank is firmly secured on the lathe, since a small piece of metal flying at high speed could be potentially lethal. If metal rod is used as a blank, a drill chuck is a suitable method of chucking. If you are turning metal between centres using a two- or four-prong drive, ensure that the tailstock is correctly tightened so that the blank cannot work free. It is also advisable to turn at a slower speed than usual, to be on the safe side.

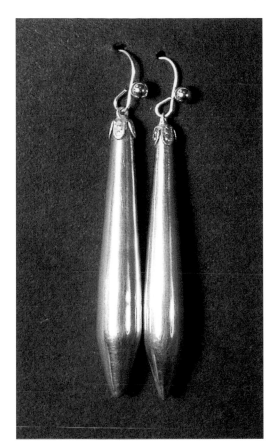

Fig 17.9 Pewter earrings.

ACRYLIC

It is possible to buy acrylic rod (sometimes referred to as Perspex) in virtually any diameter, and it is very easy to turn. It can be bought in the form of clear, solid rods which can be turned in exactly the same way as wood. Acrylic rod tends to be rather expensive to buy, so it is worth trying to obtain some off-cuts if possible. It comes in two forms: extruded and cast. The extruded variety is more difficult to turn because it has a low melting point and therefore care needs to be taken during turning and sanding to ensure that it does not melt. Cast acrylic has a higher melting point and is therefore better for turning; however care still needs to be taken even with the cast variety because turning at high speed or heavy sanding can occasionally result in surface melt.

The usual methods of chucking work well. I normally use a wooden faceplate in the method described previously on page 24.

During turning and sanding, the surface of the acrylic will take on a cloudy appearance. However, with successive sandings using finer and finer abrasive, a mirror-like finish will eventually be achieved. I usually finish with 1000 grit wet-and-dry paper (used wet), then polish using ordinary metal polish. The finished appearance resembles glass and can be extremely attractive.

During turning it produces a very strong smell of acrylic, so in addition to wearing a mask it is advisable to work in a well-ventilated room, unless a proper ventilator helmet is being worn.

Fig 17.10 Assorted items made from acrylic rod.

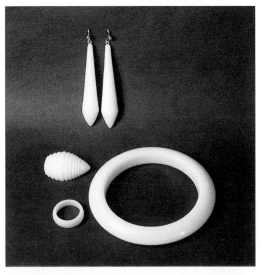

Fig 17.11 Various items turned from Corion.

143

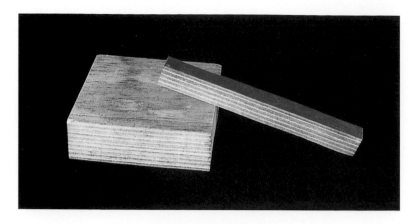

Fig 17.12 Composite-laminate blanks.

CORION

Corion is the brand name of a substance that is often used for counter tops in shops and kitchens. It resembles marble although it is actually made from an aluminium compound and acrylic. It comes in sheets about ¾in (20mm) thick and the manufacturers recommend a special glue for bonding two or more layers together. It can be obtained in a variety of pastel colours, some plain, some flecked, and is quite expensive to buy, so it is worth asking for offcuts.

It is very similar to acrylic in the way that it responds to turning. It also has a similar smell when being turned, presumably due to the acrylic content. It is soft and cuts easily and cleanly, though it does tend to blunt the tools. Finish using the same method as described for acrylic (above).

A high-gloss finish will be obtained. Corion is delightful to turn and has a very attractive surface finish when polished.

COMPOSITE COLOURED LAMINATES

Composite coloured laminates consist of blanks made up from many layers of coloured veneers that have been previously dyed in a variety of colours before being glued together (*see* Fig 17.12). The veneers are dyed, sometimes using vegetable dyes, and in some cases they are also impregnated with resin. (The latter tend to be hard to turn and produce an unpleasant resinous odour during turning.) These composite laminates are sometimes supplied under the name of 'Pakka wood' or 'Dimond wood'. They can be hard to obtain in the UK but it is possible to make one's own blanks by dyeing sycamore veneers and gluing them up to form blanks, although this is time consuming.

There are many other materials that can be turned, with varying degrees of success: alabaster, banksia nut, antler, shell, to name but a few. As always, experimentation is the key, but it is essential to observe full safety precautions and to turn slowly and carefully when turning a new material.

Fig 17.13 Bangles and earrings made from coloured composite laminate.

Appendix: Suitable Timbers

THIS SECTION LISTS a number of timbers that are suitable for jewellery from the point of view of both their aesthetic and turning qualities. Some of these, it will be noticed, are exotic/tropical varieties that are not necessarily from sustainable sources (yet). *See* page 20 for a fuller discussion of this issue.

The following is by no means an exhaustive list. Listed here in order of colour are suitable timbers that are commonly available, or that are particularly attractive. There are many other varieties that are also highly suitable for jewellery. The specific gravities given are only approximate and give an *indication* of the relative densities.

YELLOW

AMARELLO
(AKA BRAZILIAN SATINWOOD)
A bright yellow wood with uniform colour throughout; straight, fine grain; very attractive; retains its colour well.
Origin: Brazil
Specific gravity: 0.80

BOXWOOD
A yellowish wood with an extremely fine, even grain; uniform colour throughout; very dense; turns well.
Origin: Europe
Specific gravity: 0.91

LABURNUM
A green-yellow wood with attractive grain feature; tends to turn brown with age.
Origin: Europe
Specific gravity: 0.82

LEMONWOOD
(AKA CASTELLO BOXWOOD)
Very similar to boxwood (see above).
Origin: Central and South America
Specific gravity: 0.86

MULBERRY
A yellowish-brown wood with an attractive grain; tends to turn more brown with age.
Origin: Europe.
Specific gravity: 0.63

MUPANDA
(AKA OKWEN)
Similar to amarello but with a coarser grain and small dark flecks.
Origin: Africa
Specific gravity: 0.64

OSAGE
(AKA *BOIS D'ARC*)
Vivid deep yellow with striking darker stripes and a white sapwood; has a beautiful lustre and turns well; fine grained and takes a good polish; turns brown with age.
Origin: North America
Specific gravity: 0.80

PEQUIA
Very similar to amarello (see above).
Origin: South America
Specific gravity: 0.85

ORANGE

PADAUK
Colour varies according to the variety from orange-red, through brick-red to purple-brown; cream sapwood; medium grain; polishes well; turns brown with age.
Origin: Cameroon and Andaman Islands
Specific gravity (respectively): 0.72 and 0.77

TULIPWOOD
Not to be confused with North American tulipwood (see below). Although the colour is not strictly orange, it can give that appearance, being a mixture of red and yellow streaks; a very attractive timber, giving off a delightful fragrance when cut; fine grained and dense, it gives a high polish; becoming scarce due to bans on felling, and its price reflects this.
Origin: Brazil
Specific gravity: 0.96

RED/PINK

PINK IVORY
A rare timber that can be hard to acquire, due to felling bans. Its price, rightly, reflects this; bright pink in colour, with cream sapwood; extremely hard, dense, and fine grained; very attractive.
Origin: South Africa
Specific gravity: 1.04

REDWOOD PINE

A fairly soft wood, it can nevertheless be turned quite well; deep pink with attractive stripes; turns browner with age.

Origin: Scandinavia and Russia
Specific gravity: 0.40 to 0.65

ROSITA

Deep pinkish-red in colour; fine grained and very attractive; polishes well; turns browner with age.

Origin: Central America
Specific gravity: 0.74

STEAMED PEAR

Pinkish-brown with an exceptionally smooth, fine grain; uniform colour throughout; turns and polishes well.

Origin: Europe
Specific gravity: 0.70

PURPLE/BROWN

BUBINGA

An attractive red-brown wood, sometimes almost purple or with crimson streaks; fine grain, fairly dense, polishes well; similar in appearance to rosewood.

Origin: Cameroon
Specific gravity: 0.88

KINGWOOD

Very attractive wood with streaks of purple, red or brown and a cream sapwood; fine grained and very dense; polishes extremely well.

Origin: South America
Specific gravity: 1.20

PAU ROSA

Deep red-brown, often striped, with a pale sapwood; fine grained and dense, it takes a good polish.

Origin: West and East Africa
Specific gravity: 0.96

PURPLE HEART

When freshly cut, the colour is a rather dull brown, but upon exposure to light it turns a beautiful deep purple after a few days and retains this colour well; medium grain; colour and density differ according to the variety; the Colombian variety tends to be a more vivid purple than the Brazilian.

Origin: Colombia, Bolivia and Brazil.
Specific gravity (respectively): 1.1, 1.0, 0.86

ROSEWOOD

There are numerous varieties, depending on the country of origin.

All are dense, fine grained, and take a good polish; most varieties tend to be a purplish- or reddish-brown, with a pale sapwood; restrictions on most varieties, so supplies can be scarce and expensive; (some varieties are not, in fact, true rosewoods, e.g. bocote [AKA Mexican rosewood]).

Origin: Brazil, Honduras, Thailand, Indonesia, Burma and India.
Specific gravity: 0.90 (average)

WENGE

Dark brown with streaks of paler brown in an attractive pattern; a dense wood with a coarse grain.

Origin: Zaire
Specific gravity: 0.88

WHITE/OFF-WHITE/CREAM

ACACIA (AKA MYRTLE)

A creamy, yellow wood with a very attractive grain pattern; stains particularly well.

Origin: Europe and America.
Specific gravity: 0.85

HOLLY

Off-white in colour, this wood is fine grained and uniform throughout; finishes well.

Origin: Europe
Specific gravity: 0.80

HORNBEAM

A creamy, off-white timber which is very hard and dense; close grained; turns well.

Origin: Europe
Specific gravity: 0.75

SYCAMORE MAPLE

Off-white, with a uniform colour throughout; fine grained, this polishes well to give a good finish; takes stain readily; a delightful wood to turn.

Origin: Europe
Specific gravity: 0.61

TAGUA NUT (AKA VEGETABLE IVORY OR PALM NUT)

Not actually a timber but a small, roundish nut of about 1¼–1⅝in (30–40mm) diameter; it turns easily and is almost pure white in colour; used to be used for button-making; very dense, it polishes easily to a high gloss, giving it the appearance of ivory, although it is a little whiter; each nut is hollow inside.

Origin: Equador
Specific gravity: 1.20

WHITE MAPLE

A creamy-white timber of uniform colour; faint darker lines of growth rings visible; fine grained, it polishes well.

> Origin: North America
> Specific gravity: 0.72

BLACK

BLACKWOOD

There are two main varieties: African and Tasmanian; the African variety is black with a cream sapwood; very hard and dense and takes an extremely good finish; traditionally used in the manufacture of musical instruments; Tasmanian blackwood is less dense and tends to be browner in colour.

> Origin: Africa and Tasmania.
> Specific gravity (respectively):

1.2 and 0.66

EBONY

There are many different varieties of ebony; all are very hard and dense and polish to a high gloss; varieties differ in colour and appearance; African ebony is the blackest and has the most uniform colour; other varieties have varying degrees of brown or purple streaks; restricted felling and/or import bans on most varieties.

> Origin: Africa, Thailand, Indonesia, Papua New Guinea and Sabah.
> Specific gravity: 1.03 (average)

GREEN

AMERICAN TULIPWOOD (AKA YELLOW POPLAR)

Yellowish-brown with broad green bands which gradually turn brown; a light, inexpensive wood, it tends to be rather soft, making it less than ideal for turned jewellery.

> Origin: North America
> Specific gravity: 0.51

LIGNUM VITAE

This is not strictly green but has greenish streaks through parts of the timber, while the rest tends to be dark brown in colour; not an easy wood to turn, being extremely dense and oily; availability is subject to restrictions.

> Origin: West Indies and tropical America
> Specific gravity: 1.23

Bibliography

MACTAGGART, P & A *Practical Gilding* (Mac & Me Ltd, 1985)

DUGINSKE, G & M *Band Saw Basics* (Sterling, 1990)

THURSTAN, V *The Use of Vegetable Dyes* (Reeves-Dryad Press, 1977)

HARDY, WILLIAM *A Guide to Art Nouveau Style* (Quintet, 1987)

SPARKE, PENNY *Design in Context* (Quarto, 1987)

EDLIN, H E *What Wood Is That?* (Thames and Hudson Ltd, 1989)

Index

Metric Conversion Table

INCHES TO MILLIMETRES AND CENTIMETRES						
mm = millimetres cm = centimetres						
inches	mm	cm	inches	cm	inches	cm
⅛	3	0.3	9	22.9	30	76.2
¼	6	0.6	10	25.4	31	78.7
⅜	10	1.0	11	27.9	32	81.3
½	13	1.3	12	30.5	33	83.8
⅝	16	1.6	13	33.0	34	86.4
¾	19	1.9	14	35.6	35	88.9
⅞	22	2.2	15	38.1	36	91.4
1	25	2.5	16	40.6	37	94.0
1¼	32	3.2	17	43.2	38	96.5
1½	38	3.8	18	45.7	39	99.1
1¾	44	4.4	19	48.3	40	101.6
2	51	5.1	20	50.8	41	104.1
2½	64	6.4	21	53.3	42	106.7
3	76	7.6	22	55.9	43	109.2
3½	89	8.9	23	58.4	44	111.8
4	102	10.2	24	61.0	45	114.3
4½	114	11.4	25	63.5	46	116.8
5	127	12.7	26	66.0	47	119.4
6	152	15.2	27	68.6	48	121.9
7	178	17.8	28	71.1	49	124.5
8	203	20.3	29	73.7	50	127.0

About the Author

Hilary Bowen was born in Dorchester. She moved to Southampton in 1973 to study at the university, before embarking on a career in teaching. After obtaining an MA in education in 1985, she took up her current post as an education lecturer in a Southampton college of higher education.

Hilary has been woodturning for a number of years now and she is a member of both the Hampshire Woodturners' Association and the Association of Woodturners of Great Britain. Her work has been on regular display at the Northguild Art Gallery, Southampton. She has also been involved in jewellery making, which has led to her interest in combining wood and metal. It is her intention to explore the possibilities of combining wood with other materials to produce decorative effects on woodturned objects.

TITLES AVAILABLE FROM
GMC PUBLICATIONS LTD

BOOKS

Woodworking Plans and Projects	GMC Publications
40 More Woodworking Plans and Projects	GMC Publications
Woodworking Crafts Annual	GMC Publications
Woodworkers' Career and Educational	
Source Book	GMC Publications
Woodworkers' Courses and Source Book	GMC Publications
Woodturning Techniques	GMC Publications
Useful Woodturning Projects	GMC Publications
Green Woodwork	Mike Abbott
Making Little Boxes from Wood	John Bennett
Furniture Restoration and Repair	
for Beginners	Kevin Jan Bonner
Woodturning Jewellery	Hilary Bowen
The Incredible Router	Jeremy Broun
Electric Woodwork	Jeremy Broun
Woodcarving: A Complete Course	Ron Butterfield
Making Fine Furniture: Projects	Tom Darby
Restoring Rocking Horses	Clive Green and Anthony Dew
Heraldic Miniature Knights	Peter Greenhill
Practical Crafts: Seat Weaving	Ricky Holdstock
Multi-centre Woodturning	Ray Hopper
Complete Woodfinishing	Ian Hosker
Woodturning: A Source Book of Shapes	John Hunnex
Making Shaker Furniture	Barry Jackson
Upholstery: A Complete Course	David James
Upholstery Techniques and Projects	David James
The Upholsterer's Pocket Reference Book	David James

Designing and Making Wooden Toys	Terry Kelly
Making Dolls' House Furniture	Patricia King
Making and Modifying Woodworking Tools	Jim Kingshott
The Workshop	Jim Kingshott
Sharpening: The Complete Guide	Jim Kingshott
Turning Wooden Toys	Terry Lawrence
Making Board, Peg and Dice Games	Jeff and Jennie Loader
Making Wooden Toys and Games	Jeff and Jennie Loader
The Complete Dolls' House Book	Jean Nisbett
The Secrets of the Dolls' House Makers	Jean Nisbett
Wildfowl Carving, Volume 1	Jim Pearce
Make Money from Woodturning	Ann and Bob Phillips
Guide to Marketing	Jack Pigden
Woodcarving Tools, Materials and Equipment	Chris Pye
Making Tudor Dolls' Houses	Derek Rowbottom
Making Georgian Dolls' Houses	Derek Rowbottom
Making Period Dolls' House Furniture	
	Derek and Sheila Rowbottom
Woodturning: A Foundation Course	Keith Rowley
Turning Miniatures in Wood	John Sainsbury
Pleasure and Profit from Woodturning	Reg Sherwin
Making Unusual Miniatures	Graham Spalding
Woodturning Wizardry	David Springett
Adventures in Woodturning	David Springett
Furniture Projects	Rod Wales
Decorative Woodcarving	Jeremy Williams

VIDEOS

Ray Gonzalez	Carving a Figure: The Female Form
David James	The Traditional Upholstery Workshop, Part 1:
	Stuffover Upholstery
David James	The Traditional Upholstery Workshop, Part 2:
	Drop-in and Pinstuffed Seats
John Jordan	Bowl Turning
John Jordan	Hollow Turning
Jim Kingshott	Sharpening the Professional Way

Jim Kingshott	Sharpening Turning and Carving Tools
Dennis White	Woodturning:
	Part 1 Turning Between Centres
	Part 2 Turning Bowls
	Part 3 Boxes, Goblets and Screw Threads
	Part 4 Novelties and Projects
	Part 5 Classic Profiles
	Part 6 Twists and Advanced Turning

GMC Publications regularly produces new books on a wide range of woodworking and craft subjects, and an increasing number of specialist magazines, all available on subscription:

MAGAZINES

Woodcarving   Woodturning   Businessmatters

All these books and magazines are available through bookshops and newsagents, or may be ordered by post from the publishers at 166 High Street, Lewes, East Sussex BN7 1XU, telephone (01273) 477374, fax (01273) 478606.

Credit card orders are accepted.

PLEASE WRITE OR PHONE FOR A FREE CATALOGUE